ORIEL GRAY was born in Sydney in 1920. In 1937 she became a member of the Sydney New Theatre and later the Communist Party. During her time with the New Theatre she became their resident writer, organising and writing their radio show as well as writing numerous revues, agit-prop plays, one-act plays and four full length plays, all of which were performed by the New Theatre. These plays were *Marx of Time* (revue), premiered 7 June1942, *Let's Be Offensive* (revue) premiered 11 April 1943, *Lawson*, premiered 11 April 1943, *Western Limit*, premiered 21 February 1946, *My Life is My Affair* (one-act play), premiered 14 March 1947, *Had We But World Enough*, premiered 7 January 1950, *Sky Without Birds*, premiered 22 March 1951, all at Sydney New Theatre, *Drive A Hard Bargain* (one-act play), premiered 1957, Ballarat Civic Hall and *The Torrents*, 1957, Adelaide New Theatre. Oriel left the New Theatre when she left the Communist Party after becoming disillusioned with the party's policies. In 1954 *The Torrents* shared the renowned Playwright's Advisory Board prize along with Ray Lawler's *Summer of the Seventeenth Doll*. Her last play, *Burst of Summer* (produced by Irene Mitchell), won the J.C. Williamson Theatre Guild Competition in 1958. Oriel Gray has also written for radio and television. She has written scripts for *Rush* and *The Sullivans* as well as working for twelve years as a script writer on *Bellbird*. Her autobiography *Exit Left: Memoirs of a Scarlet Woman* was published in 1985 and she has since written a novel *Animal Shop*.

THE TORRENTS
BY ORIEL GRAY

Currency Press • Sydney

CURRENCY PLAYS

First published in 1988 in *Australian Women's Writing*. Penguin, Melbourne.

Published by Currency Press
PO Box 2287, Strawberry Hills NSW 2012
in 1996.

This edition first published in 2016.

The Torrents copyright © Oriel Gray, 1996, 2016; Introduction copyright © Anne-Louise Sarks, 2016

COPYING FOR EDUCATIONAL PURPOSES

The Australian *Copyright Act 1968* (Act) allows a maximum of one chapter or 10% of this book, whichever is the greater, to be copied by any educational institution for its educational purposes provided that that educational institution (or the body that administers it) has given a remuneration notice to Copyright Agency Limited (CAL) under the Act.
For details of the CAL licence for educational institutions contact CAL, Level 15/233 Castlereagh Street, Sydney, NSW, 2000; tel: within Australia 1800 066 844 toll free; outside Australia 61 2 9394 7600; fax: 61 2 9394 7601; email: info@copyright.com.au

COPYING FOR OTHER PURPOSES

Except as permitted under the Act, for example a fair dealing for the purposes of study, research, criticism or review, no part of this book may be reproduced, stored in a retrieval system, or transmitted in any form or by any means without prior written permission. All enquiries should be made to the publisher at the address above.

Any performance or public reading of *The Torrents* is forbidden unless a licence has been received from the author or the author's agent. The purchase of this book in no way gives the purchaser the right to perform the play in public, whether by means of a staged production or a reading. All applications for public performance should be addressed to Australian Literary Management, 2-A Booth St, Balmain NSW 2041, Australia; ph 61 2 9818 8557; email alphaalm8@gmail.com

Cataloguing-in-Publication data for this title is available from National Library of Australia website: www.nla.gov.au.

Typeset by Erin Dewar for Currency Press.
Cover design by Studio Emma for Currency Press.

Currency Press acknowledges the Traditional Owners of the Country on which we live and work. We pay our respects to all Aboriginal and Torres Strait Islander Elders, past and present.

Contents

Introduction	vii
Anne-Louise Sarks	
THE TORRENTS	
Act One	1
Act Two	27
Act Three	44

INTRODUCTION

Anne-Louise Sarks

Even on a first reading it's clear that Oriel Gray was a master of her craft. *The Torrents* is an elegant play. It is vivid and playful and insistent. I devoured it in one sitting. Most of all, I adored her characters—especially the women. I was thrilled by the author's audacity and courage and grieved for how little we've travelled since then.

This admiration nudged me towards the obvious question: why had this brilliant woman's work been relegated to the sidelines of the Australian theatrical canon? How could I not have heard of her? A political playwright creating complex comic roles for women is right up my theatrical alley.

I also had an immediate, if partial, answer to my own question. It is over six decades since Gray wrote *The Torrents*, and we women are still fighting for equality in our industry and on our stages. Recent announcements of the theatre seasons across Australia revealed that only 38 per cent of works programmed for 2017 were written by women. These numbers, compiled by Fairfax and Playwriting Australia, expose a real and ongoing imbalance in our theatre programming.

Oriel Gray was a pioneering political playwright—and sometime actor—born in 1920. She first began making theatre at the age of seventeen and through her prolific career wrote at least 36 works including plays, scripts for radio and television, as well as a novel and a memoir. Gray learnt her craft as the nation's first-ever Australian playwright-in-residence (at the New Theatre).

At the time Gray wrote *The Torrents* the performing arts in Australia were largely confined to imported international works. Australia was only just beginning to claim its own theatrical voice. Our country was in a period of post-War economic prosperity. A recently re-elected Robert Menzies was set to become our longest-serving Prime Minister. It was a time of material progress and cultural optimism as well as a time of anxiety, with the threat of communism looming large. The gender lines that the Second World War had temporarily blurred were being officially reinstated.

It is in this context that a talented and fiercely political female playwright wrote an Australian comedy set in the 1890s. This comedy centres around Jenny Milford, who comes to the fictional goldfield town of Koolgalla to take up a position at the local newspaper. In order to obscure her gender and secure the coveted position Jenny has used only her initials in the job application. She is well aware of the social barriers to her advancement and yet is determined to forge a life and career for herself. When 'J.G. Milford' arrives in Koolgalla and is revealed as a woman, the editor (and staff) demands her resignation. A bold Jenny convinces Rufus Norris to keep her.

> JENNY: Oh, I don't think you're hard, Mr Torrent! I think you're rather soft. Well, it is soft to get rid of someone who can be an asset to your business … and you know I can be … because you haven't the strength to be different. It's rather sad.
> RUFUS: [*livid*] I do as I see fit!
> JENNY: They said that too. 'There'll be women working everywhere in Koolgalla soon', they said—'now that Rufus Torrent has shown the way.' Oh, most of them didn't approve of the idea but they couldn't help—admiring. None of them would have had the courage to engage a woman to work for them. [*Comfortingly*] I expect it will be quite a relief to them that you hadn't, either.
>
> > RUFUS *looks at her. He appraises her move. He is moved to unwilling admiration.*

Alongside this plot runs a narrative about Koolgalla, which has almost completely exploited its gold resources and is on the precipice of a crisis. A young local entrepreneur is importuning the conservative older members of the community to recognise the town's situation and embrace a new sustainable direction for its future. *The Torrents* is a screwball comedy that, like all of Oriel's plays, has a political mission that drives the central narrative. Gray knew the power of language and believed in the potential of theatre as an instrument of change.

INTRODUCTION ix

The Torrents was not entirely unrecognised at the time. In fact it was awarded the renowned Playwrights Advisory Board (PAB) prize in 1955—one of two plays to win first prize that year. The second was Ray Lawler's *The Summer of the Seventeenth Doll*.

Both these plays mark a significant turning point in Australian theatrical history, but while *The Summer of the Seventeenth Doll* was to become central to our Australian theatrical identity *The Torrents* remained unpublished until 1988, and without professional production until 1996.

That is even more remarkable when you learn—as I did reading John McCallum's encyclopaedic and deeply insightful book *Belonging: Australian Playwriting In 20th Century*—that *The Summer of the Seventeenth Doll* only just scraped through to win its PAB prize. McCallum explains that according to Leslie Rees, who founded the PAB panel, 'the panel thought *The Torrents* the "more complete" play, but they were so impressed by the subject matter of the other play they decided it should share the prize'.

The Elizabethan Theatre Trust was established in 1955 to stage the PAB award-winners. The Trust was born out of the recognition that plays (and playwrights) can only develop and succeed in the context of performance. Both the *Doll* and *The Torrents,* as joint winners, were sent to the trust for consideration—and financial backing was offered to a production of *Doll*. It was at this moment that *Doll* began its meteoric rise while *The Torrents* disappeared into obscurity.

The Summer of the Seventeenth Doll is an important Australian play and deserving of its role in our mythology, but why didn't *The Torrents* also find its place in our theatrical canon?

Perhaps if *The Torrents* had been performed and developed further through professional production it would have. Certainly plays cannot capture our imaginations solely in their written form. Scripts need to live and breathe with an audience. But Oriel Gray never got that professional opportunity.

Why?

Was it a matter of luck? An accident of circumstance? Was Gray's work too political? Were her 'New Woman' and her bold questioning of society too dangerous for the time? Or were Gray's involvement in the political left and her previous involvement in the communist party a barrier to her acceptance by the mainstream? And of course we must ask what role Gray's gender played. In 1950 Gray was a prizewinning woman playwright with a play worthy of production. Today, Gray still has not received the critical and public recognition she deserves and *The Torrents* remains relatively unknown.

There is a convenient history—that I believe has become the dominant narrative—that there was Louis Esson and then there was nothing until there was Lawler. Oriel Gray is—or should be—a challenge to that narrative. And she is not alone. She was not the only award-winning female playwright crafting work in the '40s and '50s (many writing for theatres like the New Theatre), but almost all have remained unpublished and unperformed. Other PAB-winning playwrights such as Lynn Foster, whose play *And The Moon Will Shine* won in 1946, and Dorothy Blewett, who won in 1947 for *The First Joanna*, have been largely written out of our theatrical history. This is not because men have a unique knack and talent for crafting plays. They do, however, seem to have a knack for crafting the dominant historical narrative.

Men also have a knack for following the money. When money became a part of the Australian theatrical landscape men began to dominate—a pattern that has been observed in industries across the world. As Australian theatre moved towards a professional model— not professional in the sense of higher quality, but in the simple sense that money was involved—the ecology of Australian theatre shifted. Women playwrights who were previously as numerous as—if not more numerous than—men, simply weren't offered those same professional opportunities. It seems women were welcome to dabble in the theatre for their own amusement, but allowing them to be involved in the serious business of making art was far too risky a prospect. Even more so—one would imagine—if that work also happened to challenge the dominant cultural framework.

The transition to a professional theatre model began around the time that *The Torrents* was denied the chance of a professional production by the Elizabethan Theatre Trust. That transition has undoubtedly shaped the industry we have today, marginalised the work of women and has played a part in writing women playwrights out of Australian theatrical history.

INTRODUCTION

Oriel herself challenged the traditional Australian theatrical narrative in her memoir, *Exit Left: Memoirs of a Scarlet Woman*.

> I believe I did become a playwright in that hard winter of the forties and fifties, before *The Summer of the Seventeenth Doll*. The plays I wrote, *Lawson*, *Western Limit*, *Had We But World Enough*, *Sky Without Birds*, *The Torrents*, *Burst of Summer*, have not proved lasting, were not memorable, but I did try to hold a mirror up to my times, and sometimes I think I caught a reflection that no other writer will get because it will never be that way again. I am not ashamed of them.

It is horrible to hear this talented courageous artist speak of her work in this way. *The Torrents* is no mere period piece—it speaks to our present moment. Gray's exploration of a town that has almost exhausted its mining riches and must redefine itself to survive is uncannily relevant to Australia today. It is a play about change and how that change occurs. It's a play that argues for vision and challenges the status quo. It is an exploration of class; it grapples with questions of equality, environmental sustainability and the role of journalism in society. Gray uses Jenny Milford—her 1950s 'New Woman'—as an outsider, a figure who can question and transform a conservative community.

Oriel Gray had a talent for capturing the essence of humanity and the crisis of a society. In *The Torrents* she makes these big, complicated and fraught questions vibrant and fun without compromising the political ambition at its core. There's a lightness to Gray's writing, but always, also, an edge. It's direct and sharp and funny.

But it is Gray's characters that delight me most. And her terrific character descriptions. There's a real affection for each of her creations in her introductions:

> *A heavy step on the stairs and* RUFUS TORRENT *appears in the doorway. He is a handsome, self-possessed man about forty-eight, with thick hair and a magnificent beard, well dressed, his back flung coat displaying a rich, dark waistcoat, strung across with a heavy gold watch chain. In his deep-set eyes, curling nostril and deep-cut mouth there is pride, autocracy, exhibitionism (and withdrawal) and a big slice of charm.*

> GWYNNE *is twenty-one, very pretty and flowery. She wears a riding habit. Just now she is glancing apprehensively over her shoulder…*
>
> JENNY *comes through the doorway—neat, cool and pretty. She is aware of the odds against her, but she tries to carry it off—and it's a good try.*

Gray has given us a cast of bold characters to express her comedic flair, though with a complexity and truth that ground them. And she has gifted us two extraordinary and incredibly well-drawn women. They're smart and fierce and flawed. They're funny and robust and humble. It's such a pleasure to read Jenny and Gwynne and to watch them grow, and to delight in them challenging the men around them.

> JENNY: That's a very generous gesture, Ben! Oh, why does every man consider himself such a prize that it becomes the highest pledge of gentlemanly honour to marry the woman… yes, marry her, and patronise and belittle her for the rest of your lives together, complimenting yourselves for your divine condescension.
>
> BEN *opens his mouth to speak.*
>
> No, don't deny it! Do you wonder, then, that we—the ones you call in your contempt, the New Women—that we fight for our right to an independent wage, an independent mind, an independent life… [*Advancing on* BEN] and, one day, my fine friend, we will be condescending if we marry YOU!

Gray places her 'New Women' in 1890s country Australia and it is a radical proposition. *The Torrents* asked its 1950s audience to consider where they were, and where they might hope to be in sixty years.

> JENNY: The 'J' is for Jenny—but I always use my initials. I do not wish to take any advantage from being a woman.

Now, over sixty years since *The Torrents* was written, I'm still craving women as vivid and complex and funny as JG Milford. And I'm longing for well-crafted, entertaining plays that speak to us about who we are, and who we hope to be.

> BEN: Let me urge you to give this thing a chance. Don't pass up the future for the sake of the present that is nearly past. Don't pass up the glorious—impossible—realisable chance.

RUFUS: [*wanting to save him*] Ben…
BEN: [*wearily and emptily*] I know, Father. I sound like a fool. Excuse me gentlemen.
   At the door he turns back, bitterly.
   Oh, damn all you old—cautious—safe men. You make the world unsure!

How I wish I could start work on *The Torrents* tomorrow and spend weeks realising Gray's world and picking her brain. I'd love to talk with her about our culture and our struggles for equality, about how far we've come and how much further we have to go.

In its conclusion, *The Torrents* is collectivist. Jenny brings about great change in the local newspaper and potentially Koolgalla, but is not given credit. Nor does she seek it.

Rufus Torrent asks his son Ben in the play's final moments:

RUFUS: And who cares, in the long breadth of the years who dreamed the dream, so long as the common rest of us made it come true?
   JENNY *is looking at him and* BEN, *seeing her look, catches his breath, understanding. But* RUFUS *is looking far away.*
BEN: But Father, Jenny—
RUFUS: Jenny is more of a damned fool than I think if she cares for anything less than the achievement. She understands.

I suspect that Oriel Gray, like Jenny, cared more for the achievement than the credit. She wrote knowing full well what she was up against—as a female playwright who wrote about the challenges women faced. And yet she continued to write, into that challenge, against those obstacles, determined to make a place in the world, not so much for herself but for her work—because she believed in the potential of that work to make an impact on the world around her. Her political passion burns in all of her plays. She believed that change was possible, and that it could begin in our theatres.

What made Oriel Gray sad—and you can feel it in her comments above—was that her work did not find the audience it should have. But I am saddened too by the fact that Gray herself did not receive recognition for her courage or her talent. Instead her story has been left as a footnote to a more alluring mythology.

She deserved more.

Perhaps that is Gray's legacy—that young women are now asking these questions, and demanding their place on Australia's stages. I'm so grateful to have read her work and I hope with every fibre of my being that our nation comes to celebrate Gray as a playwright of talent and vision, and that in the not-too-distant future we honour her legacy by making her dream of a just and equal society come true.

Anne-Louise Sarks
Sydney, November 2016
Anne-Louise Sarks is a director, actor and theatre maker.

The Torrents was first produced at Stow Hall by the Adelaide New Theatre on 9 August 1956 with the following cast:

CHRISTY	Frank Gargo
BERNIE	Peter Kinnane
JOCK MCDONALD	Fred Cannon
GWYNNE	Fay Cowling
KINGSLEY MYERS	Don Tilmouth
RUFUS TORRENT	Barry McEwin
BEN TORRENT	John Aust
J.G. MILFORD	Pamela Jeffries
MR MANSON	Herbert Thompson
STUWELL SNR	Sid Reid
CHARLIE (STUWELL JNR)	Keith Hall
MR SQUIRES	Brian Fisher
MR TWIMPLE	Rex Munn

Produced by Mary Miller
Set design and painting, Lindsay Wark
Costumes, Ann Neill
Lights, John Dawson
Stage manager, Frank Mueller

CHARACTERS

CHRISTY, old, gnomish, fantastic

BERNIE, aged sixteen, gauche, with a puppy charm

JOCK MCDONALD, fifty-years-old, very hard and stringy, a sharp voice, a Scots accent, a shrewd, competent fair-minded man

GWYNNE THOMAS, twenty-one, very pretty and flowery

KINGSLEY MYERS, a sturdy, good-humoured, pleasant-faced, downright young man

RUFUS TORRENT, a handsome, self-possessed man about forty-eight, with thick hair and a magnificent beard

BEN TORRENT, Rufus' son. Handsome, beguiling, a little spoilt, somewhat in awe of his father

J.G. MILFORD [JENNY], neat, cool and pretty

JOHN MANSON, an arrogant, forceful man, who can hide his ruthlessness in earthy good-fellowship, or display it when he chooses

STUWELL SNR, leading storekeeper—rather pompous

CHARLIE [STUWELL JNR], his bored son

MR SQUIRES, a shrewd rather mean little man

MR TWIMPLE, pleasant but ineffectual

ACT ONE

SCENE ONE

The office of the Koolgalla Argus. *The larger part of the set is occupied by an all-purpose room. It is in a dreadful muddle—on the small table downstage right, there are several green baize boxes, bursting at their sides, spilling blocks on to the floor. There is a scratched and bow-legged desk with a typewriter of the period, and a collection of newspaper files. There is also a filing cabinet, and a branching Victorian-type hat-rack... empty at the moment. A door marked 'PRIVATE' leads into Rufus Torrent's office... a small area (preferably on a slightly higher level), furnished with an imposing desk and swivel chair... (all we can see of it).*

Except for the dust and the untidiness, the impression of the set is warm and light—windows look down on the main street of Koolgalla.

On one wall is a dusty glass case carrying a plaster cast of a nugget—the first great find in the district. There is also a calendar, which displays— amid a quantity of scrollwork—a picture resembling the 'Stag at Bay', and the beginning of the year '189-' (the last digit torn off). There is also a picture of Queen Victoria—to which has been added a long, curly moustache.

As the curtain rises, CHRISTY—*old, gnomish, fantastic—is perched on the desk upstage, spinning a yarn to* BERNIE, *who is sixteen, gauche, with a puppy charm. The feeling of the scene is that of the schoolroom picture of the old sailor telling stories to young Raleigh and Frobisher...*

CHRISTY: [*this is pure showmanship*] O' course, we all knew there was goin' to be trouble—there had to be. 'By Grundy', says Jim Stephens to me... he was a mate of mine, little feller with a wall eye... 'nuther feller I knew had a piebald gelding with an eye the very spit of Jim's.

BERNIE: [*anxious to get on with the story*] And then Jim Stephens said to you—

CHRISTY: Eh? Oh yes—'By Grundy', he says, 'if the red coats take the Reform League lying down, we'll be able to use 'em for doormats!' O' course, we knew they wouldn't, but—'Let 'em come', we said!

BERNIE: [*awed and believing*] And you really knew Peter Lalor, Christy?

CHRISTY: [*with a light laugh*] Knew 'im? Well as I know you, young Bernie! 'Christy', he used to say, 'Christy, you're only the size of half a man, but by Grundy, you're worth ten!' He had a quaint way of expressing himself—Irish he was, y'know like his Nibs…

Thumbing a gesture towards the door marked 'PRIVATE'.

BERNIE: And were you there when they took—the Oath?

CHRISTY: Was I there? By Grundy, I… well, I wasn't exactly there, because I was called away on business that day, but there was—oh, now, how many would it be… a thousand say—or maybe eight hundred…

BERNIE: Five hundred, Christy…

CHRISTY: As I was saying—five hundred…

BERNIE: [*softly: he knows it by heart and he lives it as he speaks*] Five hundred armed diggers then assembled, and Peter Lalor was on the stump, holding with his left hand the muzzle of his rifle. A gesture of his right hand signified what he meant when he said, 'It is my duty now to swear you in'.

JOCK MACDONALD *appears in the doorway—a man of fifty, very hard and stringy, a sharp voice, a Scots accent, a shrewd, competent fair-minded man. He watches and listens, half annoyed, half amused.* CHRISTY *and* BERNIE *are quite unaware of him.*

Lalor now knelt, with head uncovered, and with the right hand pointing to the standard, exclaimed in a firm measured tone.

JOCK: Get those proofs pulled up!

CHRISTY *and* BERNIE *both jump.* CHRISTY *gets down from the desk.* BERNIE *looks shamefaced.*

When I tell you to do a job, Bernie, I trust you—I don't expect to have to be calling you every ten minutes, like a mother with a bairn in leading-strings. Now we're waiting for those proofs, and they're

ACT ONE 3

no' pulled yet, and the third page can't be locked up until they are.
BERNIE: I'm sorry, Mr MacDonald, but Christy began to tell me...
JOCK: [*sternly*] How old are you, Bernie?
BERNIE: Nearly sixteen.
JOCK: Old enough to be working—old enough to take responsibility.
BERNIE: I've been hard at it since early this morning, Mr MacDonald.
JOCK: If you don't like it, my lad, get your mother's washing up dish and start panning for gold like the rest of the town boys. You wanted to be a journalist—you begged me to get you this position—I swore to Mr Torrent that you'd justify me...
BERNIE: I'm going to, Mr MacDonald, but... but...
JOCK: But what?
BERNIE: [*blurting it out*] Sorting type and greasing blocks and delivering proofs is an awful long way from being a proper journalist like Ben Torrent.
JOCK: Indeed? And how do you think Ben Torrent—aye, and his father, too—learned to be 'proper' journalists except by sorting type, and greasing blocks and delivering proofs.
BERNIE: [*defensively*] Anyway, I thought you might be holding the proofs until the new reader starts work so's he could check them and...
JOCK: [*sweeping over him*] I tell you, Bernie, being a journalist isn't lounging in court with a flower in your buttonhole and liquor on your breath like some city fellows. If a man canna get a story, write it, set it up, print it—aye, and sell the paper if he has to—if he canna do that, then he's not good enough for the *Koolgalla Argus*—or Rufus Torrent—or me! Now away to those proofs!

Abashed, BERNIE *goes off at a fast slink.*

[*Turning his wrath on* CHRISTY] As for you, Christy, you ought to be ashamed of yourself, tempting the lad from his work with your lying stories...
CHRISTY: [*indignant*] Now that's a libel if ever I heard one! We was talking about the Eureka Stockade.
JOCK: I suppose you were there, too... carrying the banner, most like.
CHRISTY: [*virtuously*] I never...
JOCK: If they had stood the flagstaff in a barrel of beer, then you would

never have left it, that's certain! Fifty-four—wasn't that the year you told me you were in Queensland as an officer of the Native Police, holding the wild blacks at bay, and sleeping across the doorway of the Governor's lady's bedroom.

CHRISTY: [*unabashedly*] So it was—and me wishing I was on the other side. By Grundy, Jock she was a fine figure of a woman...

JOCK: None of that talk in front of the lad—he's drowsy enough already! Get to your work you old he-goat... and hurry!

> JOCK *bellows this at* CHRISTY. CHRISTY *is unmoved, but* GWYNNE THOMAS *is startled.* GWYNNE *is twenty-one, very pretty and flowery. She wears a riding habit. Just now she is glancing apprehensively over her shoulder, and* CHRISTY *takes advantage of this to steady her, his little eyes gleaming as he grabs her slim waist.*

CHRISTY: Watch it now, Gwynne, or you'll be tail over turkey...!

> JOCK *glares, and* CHRISTY *vanishes from sight.*

JOCK: That Christy...! I think Mr Torrent keeps him for the joke of him. Mind you, he can work if he's got a mind to it—it's getting his mind to it that baffles you!

> KINGSLEY MYERS *comes in, as though he has run up the stairs. He is a sturdy, good-humoured, pleasant-faced, downright young man, and at the moment, he is annoyed.*

KINGSLEY: Gwynne, why did you snub me just now?

GWYNNE: I didn't see you—I mean—I did but—

> JOCK *coughs.* GWYNNE *indicates him.*

Mr MacDonald's here, Kingsley...

> KINGSLEY *shuts up, but he only postpones what he has to say.*

JOCK: You'll be looking for Ben, Miss Thomas?

GWYNNE: Oh, no... The city train's not in yet.

JOCK: [*surprised*] Ben came back yesterday, with everything arranged. The new man's following on this morning's train...

GWYNNE: [*surprised, hiding it*] Oh... oh, yes, of course, how silly of me... He told me—last night—

> KINGSLEY *looking at her.*

ACT ONE

[*Hastily*] You'll be glad to see the new staff member, Mr MacDonald.
JOCK: I will that. Bernie's a good lad, but Christy and I've been fairly worked off our feet—I should say Christy's been worked off my feet! Once this new chap's settled in, Mr Torrent'll take on more staff. He's promised.
GWYNNE: Koolgalla's really expanding—that's what my father says.
KINGSLEY: Oh, Koolgalla's bursting at the seams—wait for the bang when the gold runs out!

JOCK gives him a shrewd look.

JOCK: That's a real hobby horse of yours, Mr Myers. A real queer one for an engineer.
KINGSLEY: I'm only an engineer by second choice... It's the land and the saving of it that I love— [*He looks to* GWYNNE.] among other things.

JOCK is aware of the tension.

JOCK: I'll be away...

JOCK goes out. GWYNNE starts to flutter after him.

GWYNNE: Mr MacDonald, I'll come back...

KINGSLEY *catches her by the wrist.*

KINGSLEY: I won't eat you, Gwynne.

GWYNNE *clutches at her dignity.*

GWYNNE: I have never considered that...
KINGSLEY: That I love you?

She shakes her head.

You're too honest to lie well, Gwynne.
GWYNNE: I don't lie!
KINGSLEY: No? Not even when you try to hide the fact that Ben came back last night and didn't come to see you?

GWYNNE *pulls her hand away.*

GWYNNE: [*attacking him*] I thought you were his friend?
KINGSLEY: I am his friend—as much as Ben Torrent needs a friend. But I'm tired of being 'mates'. There are things I want—and not just for myself. I've a right to fight for them.

GWYNNE: I'm to marry Ben—soon.

> KINGSLEY *turns away… she follows him. She really doesn't want to let him go.*

KINGSLEY: Because his father thinks it's a good idea—because your father thinks it's a good idea? Oh, I know how it's done—a marriage has been arranged. It's barbaric—one Hottentot chief to another!

> GWYNNE *touches his shoulder.*

GWYNNE: Please, King…

KINGSLEY: Don't think you're my only heart's desire! I want to bring water from the river to the paddocks out there! I want to hold the river against drought and flood. I want to see fruit trees, instead of mine shafts and pot-holes. [*Savagely*] I've got as much chance of that as I have of you. But I haven't given up!

GWYNNE: This is gold country—Father says it's rich…

KINGSLEY: It was rich. Riches run out like the wrong kind of love.

GWYNNE: You mustn't talk like this. I'm to marry Ben…

KINGSLEY: Different people love in different ways. Some people love dangerously and carelessly—living for themselves, as much as they live for each other. That's their way, and I won't quarrel with it. That's Ben's way, Gwynne—but it's not yours.

> KINGSLEY *takes* GWYNNE's *hands. She is very drawn to him.* CHRISTY *comes in with some proofs. His eyes pop from one to the other as* GWYNNE *turns away sharply.*

CHRISTY: Didn't mean to make you jump—move like a cat—can't help it. Trained myself to it, you know, in Queensland commanding a troop of native police, I was. Oho, they were a wild lot, too—kept 'em in order with the threat of a flogging and, the promise of rum…

> JOCK's *voice is heard downstairs… sturdily respectful.*

JOCK: Good morning to ye, Mr Torrent.

> BERNIE's *voice chimes in on top of this, calling upstairs.*

BERNIE: Good morning, Mr Torrent.

> *A heavy step on the stairs and* RUFUS TORRENT *appears in the doorway. He is a handsome, self-possessed man about forty-eight,*

ACT ONE

with thick hair and a magnificent beard, well dressed, his back flung coat displaying a rich, dark waistcoat, strung across with a heavy gold watch chain. In his deep-set eyes, curling nostril and deep-cut mouth there is pride, autocracy, exhibitionism (and withdrawal) and a big slice of charm. As he enters the room his quick glance takes in GWYNNE *and* KINGSLEY… *there is no suspicion in it, just his usual observation.* CHRISTY *greets him.*

CHRISTY: By God and by Grundy, it's a fine morning, Mr Torrent.

RUFUS: [*jovially*] So good that God will forgive even the blasphemy, Christy. These proofs for me?

He takes them.

Ah, Gwynne, my dear—and as pretty as the morning itself…

In moments like these, RUFUS' *brogue, usually carefully controlled, suggests itself.*

Good morning, Kingsley. Christy, remind Mr MacDonald to keep an extra half column open for the court stories, will you? Judge Shaw expects to adjourn early this morning, so Ben should be in at any moment.

CHRISTY *nods and shuffles off.* RUFUS *starts across room to hat stand on which he hangs his glossily dignified hat. He looks over his shoulder.*

Did Kingsley have to act as your escort, Gwynne?

GWYNNE *is embarrassed and that annoys* KINGSLEY.

I hope Ben hears of it… make him envious… keep him up to the mark.

GWYNNE: [*hastily*] King… Mr Myers and I met here…

RUFUS: Do you want to see me—or Ben—Kingsley?

KINGSLEY: May I see you, sir…?

The coolness intended for GWYNNE *reacts on her—and on* RUFUS.

RUFUS: Well, that sounds serious. You don't want to see me, do you, Gwynne?

GWYNNE: Oh, no… I mean…

RUFUS: [*joking*] You mean, I'm not the right Torrent.
GWYNNE: How is Ben this morning, Mr Torrent?
> *She is wondering where* BEN *spent last night.*

RUFUS: I haven't seen him. For once, he had risen early, and had gone before I came down to breakfast—so Mrs. Preston told me. I haven't even had the opportunity to question him about our new colleague, all he would say was that I was completely justified in the favourable impression I was given by his application... clear, concise. [*To* GWYNNE] Did Ben give you any information, my dear?
GWYNNE: No, Mr Torrent.
RUFUS: I thought he might have said something last night—but then, young lovers who have been separated have more things to talk about, I imagine... don't you, Kingsley?
KINGSLEY: I've never given the matter any thought, sir.
> RUFUS *shoots him a questioning glance...* RUFUS *is never so intent on himself or his business that he loses his awareness of small things.*

GWYNNE: Good morning, Mr Torrent.
RUFUS: Goodbye, my dear. I'll tell Ben...
> GWYNNE *shoots a troubled glance in* KINGSLEY*'s direction and her 'Good morning' trailing away is meant for* KINGSLEY. *He knows it, but is still annoyed enough to ignore her. She goes.* RUFUS *moves through into his private office. He is surprised when* KINGSLEY *follows him in.*

KINGSLEY: Can I see you for a minute, sir?
RUFUS: Close the door.
> KINGSLEY *does so. He is rather bitter in his approach in this scene.*

KINGSLEY: Not that what I've got to say is very private—I talk too much when I'm enthusiastic. Mr Manson often has a bit of fun at my expense. We were having a drink in the Travellers' Arms, and he got someone to go out and buy a kid's tin bucket and he gave it to me full of beer... 'Here you are, Kingsley,' he said. 'Feed this into your irrigation scheme.'
> RUFUS *warms to* KINGSLEY *because he loathes* MANSON *himself.*

Well—that's Mr Manson… a wealthy man, an influential man—but not one to look to for understanding. Rufus, can I look to you for it? You're a man of integrity—a man of vision.

RUFUS: I'm also a man who runs a newspaper, my boy, and my directors, with good money sunk in those mines out there, will be screaming like banshees—if you comprehend the term—if I come out in support of your scheme.

    KINGSLEY's *mouth opens in further argument,* RUFUS *halts him.*

Besides, I'm not—really—convinced, Kingsley… Koolgalla is a gold town. Oh, I know it isn't as prosperous as it has been—but all the interests here—big and small—are sunk in gold, and it's still paying off.

KINGSLEY: For the moment. The big interests…

RUFUS: I said big and small. And the small people will be against you, too, if you ask them to give up their dreams of Eldorado, their hope of swift and easy fortune. What can you give them in its place?

KINGSLEY: Real hope—not chance, and a blind stab in the dark. I tell you, Mr Torrent, bring water to this land and it will grow anything—peaches this size, melons, grapes. With water, we can—

RUFUS: But we have water—

KINGSLEY: [*scornfully*] Yes—for the gold sluices—a muddy trickle in the dry spells and a roaring torrent in the floods. Look sir, this isn't only for Koolgalla. If this scheme is successful, we can prove to the rest of the country—[*He pulls up short; stiffly.*] I suppose you think I'm an egotist seeking applause—

RUFUS: [*his warmth and charm very apparent*] Worse, King—I think you're a self-sacrificer. People will follow an egotist sooner, because his sense of self-preservation gives them confidence. With a self-sacrificer, they're afraid that they may get caught up in his particular martyrdom.

KINGSLEY: [*brushing this aside*] And you won't help me?

RUFUS: I can make it possible for you to lay your scheme before the town Council.

KINGSLEY: I've seen them…

RUFUS: You can talk to my directors at their next meeting—try to win their support.

KINGSLEY: Thanks—I will. But you won't back me personally—advocate the scheme yourself... ?

RUFUS: [*after a moment—understanding* KINGSLEY*'s disappointment*] No, Kingsley.

> With a hopeless gesture, KINGSLEY *turns away and is about to pick up his hat when* BEN TORRENT *comes in.* BEN *is young, handsome, beguiling, a little spoilt, somewhat in awe of his father, and certainly dominated by* RUFUS' *authority and leadership. Despite the warm morning, he wears a dark overcoat buttoned up to his throat and carries a soft dark felt hat which he tosses on to the desk.*

[*Glad of the interruption*] Good morning, Ben.

BEN: Good morning, Father... Hello, King.

KINGSLEY: How is crime in Koolgalla, Ben?

BEN: Prospering.

RUFUS: What's wrong with you, boy—wrapped round in that heavy overcoat, with summer outside the window. Take it off.

> BEN *gathers the coat closer round his throat.*

BEN: I feel the cold, Father. I think I have a chill.

RUFUS: [*good humoured, but patronising*] I don't know what's wrong with the young men today. They're all becoming effete. Perhaps it's the warm climate here that makes their blood run thin. Now when I lived in Dublin—oh, those winter morning and the grey evenings, standing on the street corners, clenching your hands in the torn pockets of your overcoat, watching the girls coming from the factories, with their shawls folded over their beautiful bright heads... [*He stops himself suddenly, aware of the others' interest. Austerely.*] It made a man of me.

BEN: The weather, Father—or the girls?

RUFUS: Ben, you have a frivolous turn of mind. You know, Kingsley, I wonder did I do right to trust Ben to engage our new colleague...

BEN: [*hastily*] May I remind you, Father—you had made your decision already.

RUFUS: Nonsense—I left it entirely to you. I did happen to remark that from the applications received... we had quite a number, Kingsley... Koolgalla must have become more than a fly-by-night village…

BEN: It will become much less, once the gold runs out.

RUFUS: [*testily*] As I say, I did remark that, judging from qualifications stated, J.G. Milford…

BEN: [*with a curious satisfaction*] Seemed by far the most suitable—yes, you did. And having interviewed the others we had considered, I was forced—forced, Father—to your point of view. And J.G. Milford arrives by today's train.

RUFUS: That should be in soon—we must meet it.

BEN: I'll attend to that.

RUFUS: Is he very fast?

BEN: Oh, I don't think—Oh, you mean the—the typing—and shorthand. Very, Father—and accurate—reads and marks proofs clearly…

RUFUS: [*pleased with himself*] I knew—there was a ring of truthfulness. And the letter, Kingsley—a really well-written business letter. Not too many men can write a good business letter. Yes, I think this Milford will be just what we need here.

BEN: That is your considered opinion, Father?

RUFUS: Certainly.

BEN: I'm glad of that.

> BERNIE *comes in.*

BERNIE: Excuse me, Mr Torrent. Mr MacDonald asked had you checked that proof?

RUFUS: I've got it here… [*As* BERNIE *holds out his hand*] No I'll come down for a moment. Don't forget that train, Ben—we don't want to seem unfriendly. [*Jovially to* BERNIE *as he follows him out*] You'll have to be wide-awake now, Bernie—mustn't let this city gentleman think he's paddled his canoe into a backwater, eh…

> *He has gone, in the sound of his own chuckle and* BERNIE*'s flattered 'No, Mr Torrent'.* KINGSLEY, *still glum, is lounging in the window left, and* BEN *is standing at the desk, his back to the audience.*

KINGSLEY: Ben, I talked to your father...

> BEN *turns round to face him. Now his coat is open and thrown back and under it, he is still in handsome but slightly rumpled dress clothes.*

[*Really laughing*] Ben—you fool! You haven't been home all night!
BEN: Straight to court—and on the hottest morning this year! Even the judge was looking at me, as he sat with his gown thrown back as far as decorum allowed...
KINGSLEY: But your father said you'd had breakfast...?
BEN: Mrs Preston always hides me from the Wrath. I have a way with housekeepers.
KINGSLEY: [*sighing*] You have a way with any female. Gwynne— [*Stumbling*] your fiancée—has been here looking for you...
BEN: Oh, hell! Did she say anything to Father about me not seeing her yesterday?
KINGSLEY: [*sternly*] No. She let him think you had.
BEN: I meant to—I met someone. Is Gwynne very annoyed?
KINGSLEY: She is hurt.
BEN: [*groans*] Much worse. Dammit, King, why does one have anything to do with nice women. The not-nice ones are so much less expensive in the long run. They do give something in return for payment. Nice women take everything from you, and still leave you feeling you owe them something... it might be your heart, or your brain, or your soul—or your sins. And they are the hardest things to give up!
KINGSLEY: [*who can be very Victorian*] Perhaps we men forget what good women sacrifice for us.
BEN: [*lighting a cigarette—*KINGSLEY *refuses one with a head shake*] They never allow us to do that!
KINGSLEY: It's a pity you're so plagued with women, Ben—but you must turn to one kind or the other.
BEN: [*smiling*] You like Gwynne—very much—don't you?
KINGSLEY: [*stiffly*] I admire and venerate Miss Thomas...
BEN: You sound like the inscription on a tombstone! Gwynne is a perfect darling... [*Meaning it*] You know, if you really care, King—I wouldn't stand in your way—
KINGSLEY: [*for whom the morning has been too much*] I wouldn't, Ben—stand in my way at this moment, or I'll punch your nose...

> *As* BEN *is staring, and* KINGSLEY *glaring,* RUFUS *comes back in,* BEN *struggles to engulf himself in the coat,* KINGSLEY *to hold* RUFUS' *attention.*

ACT ONE 13

RUFUS: Ben, you're still wrapped in that coat…
KINGSLEY: [*babbling, looking out of the window*] Big crowd in the streets, Mr Torrent… wonderful view you've got from these windows…

> RUFUS *is looking suspiciously from one young man to the other. He knows they are hiding something.*

There's old Stuwell—and his son.

> RUFUS *walks over behind him and looks out.*

I tell you, Mr Torrent, if you want to try to talk sense to two stupid people…
RUFUS: My directors…

> KINGSLEY, *turning his head and finding himself face to face with* RUFUS, *decides to look out again.*

KINGSLEY: Now I know why there is such a crowd in the streets… the train's in early…
BEN: [*enshrouded in his coat again*] The train's in! Oh, damnation… I meant to meet—
RUFUS: Not much of a welcome for the new man, Ben.

> JOHN MANSON *walks in. Physically, he is a worthy opponent for* RUFUS—*an arrogant, forceful man, who can hide his ruthlessness in earthy good-fellowship, or display it when he chooses. He has no son—this increases his dislike for* RUFUS. *His manner to* BEN *is indulgent, and even in disagreement, it is flattering. He would love to win* BEN *to some enterprise.* MANSON *is not noticed at first.* BEN *is half-delighted, half apprehensive about what he has done.*

BEN: Oh, I'll explain. The new employee will understand… very understanding, the new employee. I hope you'll feel the same way, Father.
RUFUS: [*irritably*] Don't babble, Ben—
MANSON: That's how a young man feels on a fine morning… like breakfasting on bubbly—

> BEN *is thrown off balance.*

BEN: Oh, hell!… You here!

MANSON: Now what's wrong with me, Ben?

BEN: I didn't know Mr Manson would be here, Father. [*Meaning, I didn't mean to pull this in front of him.*] You see—J.G. Milford may be something of a surprise.

> CHRISTY *appears in the doorway, clutching the suitcases. He drops a suitcase, jerks a thumb over his shoulder.*

CHRISTY: S'here… !

RUFUS: Christy, you've been drinking!

CHRISTY: By Grundy, I ain't—but by God, I'm goin' to… and I'll take a bet that I'm not the only one. J—G—MILFORD!

> JENNY *comes through the doorway—neat, cool and pretty. She is aware of the odds against her, but she tries to carry it off—and it's a good try. Faces seen.* JENNY *looks to* BEN. RUFUS *looks murder at* BEN.

RUFUS: J.G. Milford…

JENNY: The 'J' is for Jenny—but I always use my initials. I do not wish to take any advantage from being a woman.

> MANSON *roars with laughter.*

MANSON: Ben, I congratulate you. Ben certainly took you there, Torrent.

> JENNY *looks at him.*

John Manson, ma'am…

> JENNY *ducks her head in acknowledgement. She looks to* RUFUS. *She is inwardly quaking.* CHRISTY, *at entrance, has been joined by* JOCK. BEN *inches towards exit.*

BEN: Remember, Father—your considered opinion.

> *As the curtain comes down,* JENNY *is looking from one to the other.* RUFUS *is still glaring at* BEN.

The lowered curtain marks a time lapse.

The office of the Koolgalla Argus. *Late afternoon, same day.* KINGSLEY *feels rather awkward, but also feels Victorian—protective about* GWYNNE. GWYNNE *shows more spark than she did in the morning—*

ACT ONE

less of the ideal of Victorian girlhood… in fact, she is angry with BEN. BEN, *dressed in a day suit now, his hat on the back of his head, is both noncommittal and provoking, the way he often is when he knows he's been rather outrageous. He moves about the set a lot, sits on the edge of the desk, examines blocks, is impudent, cajoling, stubborn in turn.*

GWYNNE: Where is she now?

BEN: Settling into her room in Mrs. Crabtree's boarding house I suppose…

GWYNNE: Don't you know… ?

> BEN *gets enormously interested in a proof. Unconsciously,* GWYNNE *is relying on* KINGSLEY *as her supporter, so she looks at him.*

Why did you do it, Ben?

KINGSLEY: You must have been out of your mind.

BEN: You're so keen on irrigation, King. I'm irrigating the intellectual stream. I'm tossing a stone in the pool of reflection. I've often said I wanted something to change in Koolgalla…

GWYNNE: How could you be taken in by someone like that—writing all those lies!

BEN: What lies? She has done everything she claimed in her letter.

GWYNNE: But she's a woman!

BEN: Her father was an editor of a paper in Tasmania—a paper very like the *Argus*. He didn't have a son—and since he had liberal ideas… if either of you can understand that expression—

KINGSLEY: Steady on, Ben—

BEN: He wanted his daughter to be something more than a fashion-plate—or a queen bee!

GWYNNE: You mean that for me.

BEN: You always say I don't explain things to you… now, I'm explaining. Miss Milford acted in much the same capacity to her father as I do to mine.

KINGSLEY: Fair enough perhaps—in Tasmania. But it's rather much to expect Koolgalla to take.

BEN: So is your irrigation scheme. Gwynne, shall I see you home?

GWYNNE: No, thank you, Ben. If Rainbird hadn't thrown a shoe, I wouldn't have come back here today.

KINGSLEY: I could ride that way…
GWYNNE: Thank you, King…

> *She is quite angry.*

[*To* BEN] I'm sure that will be suitable to you… ?

> *She looks at* BEN. *She is still in love with him, would like to provoke him into making some claim on her.* KINGSLEY *waits, too, then says…*

KINGSLEY: I'll—get the horses from the livery stable—

> KINGSLEY *goes out. The light is dying, and there is a soft sunset light in the office.* BEN *turns to her with momentary remorse.*

BEN: Gwynne, I don't mean…
GWYNNE: What, Ben?
BEN: I don't mean to be—me, I suppose.

> *He puts his arms around her.*

But you know what I am.
GWYNNE: [*sadly*] No, I don't know what you are. I don't even know if you want to marry me.

> BEN *is really fond of* GWYNNE, *attracted to her sweetness and prettiness. They kiss—quite fervently—but* GWYNNE *draws away. To look at him.*

You do want to marry me, Ben?

> BEN *turns his head, to listen to a sound.*

BEN: Yes, pet, but it may not be possible. You may be a widow before you're a bride! Father has just come in.
GWYNNE: Oh, Ben, can't you give this woman some money and make her go away again?
BEN: Is that your solution? No—I can't.

> RUFUS *walks in. He is still in a controlled fury. He unbends to* GWYNNE.

RUFUS: Gwynne, my dear… I didn't expect to see you in town still.
GWYNNE: Rainbird cast a shoe.

> RUFUS *is longing to get at* BEN, *but ladies must come first.*

ACT ONE

RUFUS: Well... I do want to see you, Ben, after you have taken Gwynne home.
GWYNNE: [*a touch of feline*] Ben thought you would want to talk to him. Nothing must stand in the way of that!

> RUFUS *looks at* BEN. BEN *looks back, defiant.*

Goodnight, Mr Torrent.
RUFUS: Will you never learn to call me 'Papa'... That is what I will be when you and Ben are married.
GWYNNE: I think it would be very difficult to think of you as 'Papa'...

> GWYNNE *goes out.*

RUFUS: [*a bit flattered*] And now, Ben, have you any explanation?
BEN: Yes, sir—your considered opinion. J.G. Milford was your choice.
RUFUS: I left it to you...
BEN: You didn't leave it to me, Father. You had made your decision before I ever left Koolgalla. Had I come back with any other applicant, you would have considered my decision ill-advised. You'll just have to put up with it, Father—that the 'J' is for Jenny.

SCENE TWO

The office. One week later, about lunch time. It looks much as before, but the desk with the typewriter is tidy, the blocks have been stacked neatly in the mended boxes, the files placed neatly inside them. On the hat rack RUFUS' *hat sits square and determinedly over the very top of the rack itself.*

RUFUS *is standing in the doorway of his inner office listening to* CHRISTY, *who is holding the floor.* JOCK MACDONALD *leans up against the desk and* BERNIE *is standing rather timidly near the doorway.*

CHRISTY: By Grundy, I said to her... By Grundy, I been in the printing business for fifty years, I said! I have been, too! Started when I was as young as young Bernie here... used to work for a couple of brothers in Jindabyne; twins, they were—like a couple of peas. You know, a funny thing happened the time Jim got married to Elsie Wainwright...

JOCK: Stick to the subject, Christy. That has nothing to do with Miss Milford.

CHRISTY: Well, I was just telling you that I was telling her that I'd been in the printing game for fifty years...

JOCK: When you were not chasing outlaw blacks and fighting on the Eureka Stockade and...

CHRISTY: [*a quick glance at* BERNIE... CHRISTY *doesn't want to lose his audience there. Dignified.*] Fifty years—on and off. And in that time I says to her, nobody has ever told me that my type needed cleaning—and nobody's ever going to make me clean it! Furthermore, I says to her, when I took the next proof up, furthermore, now that it has been cleaned, I defy you to tell me that you can spot any difference!

RUFUS: But you cleaned it?

CHRISTY: [*taken aback*] Just to prove my point though!

JOCK: [*who can't resist baiting* CHRISTY] He cleaned it all right, Mr Torrent... the lassie tricked him into that finally!

CHRISTY: Taking her side, you old petticoat-chaser? 'Mister Christy' she calls me! Mister!

BERNIE: She might mean to be polite, Christy.

CHRISTY: [*getting himself annoyed*] And who is she... her with her pink blouse and her sailor hat, to come being polite to Christy Blades? Furthermore, I said to her, by God, a woman's place is in the home!

JOCK: [*surprised by this phrase. Even* RUFUS *nods approval*] That's verra well put... oreaginal...

CHRISTY: [*basking in the approval*] Oh, I ain't been putting words together at a frame for fifty years without learning how to string a couple together in my head. I remember one time I was working on a newspaper—

RUFUS: [*deciding this has gone far enough*] So from all this, I gather that you men are not at all contented to continue working here with Miss Milford?

> BERNIE *would love to speak out but just can't manage it.* JOCK *hesitates.*

JOCK: We-ll, Mr Torrent... It's not so much us. But you mind those new men you promised we'd be getting...

> RUFUS *is amused... he knows this is blackmail.*

ACT ONE

RUFUS: I haven't forgotten, Jock. Just as soon as this matter is settled.
JOCK: We might manage to rub along with the lass—
BERNIE: Oh, yes… !

He gets quenching looks from the others.

JOCK: —but if we've got the new men to consider—they might not care to work with a lady.
RUFUS: We have all worked together here so harmoniously in the past that I would not like to see that harmony upset… If you wish it, when Miss Milford returns from her lunch, I will put your objections before her.

JENNY has walked in. She takes the situation in—she has been waiting for something like this. She comes as a shock to them, even to RUFUS.

Oh—Miss Milford, Jock and Christy came to see me on this question of your continued employment here… you remember… a trial period… ?
JOCK: Well, Mr Torrent, it was you that came and asked for our opinion.
RUFUS: I felt it was my duty to discover the feelings of the rest of my staff. They—have an objection…
JENNY: You mean you would like my resignation?
BERNIE: Oh, no… !

He gets glared at by everybody.

RUFUS: Thank you, Miss Milford…
JENNY: I shan't give it!

General stupefaction!

Has my work been so unsatisfactory?
RUFUS: On the contrary, you are very efficient. When you leave us, Miss Milford, I will be happy to give you the best of references. I shall simply say that circumstances over which we had no control necessitated your resignation… and that any future employer will be gaining an asset—
JENNY: So long as he has more control over the circumstances.
RUFUS: Shall we be honest, Miss Milford—
JENNY: I would prefer it.

RUFUS: A printing office of a newspaper is no place for a member of the female sex. It is a place for men of the world—violent and terrible happenings are its very life's blood. There is no protection for natural womanly weakness. Sometimes, the language—the language is not fit for your ears.

JENNY: Then you should all be ashamed! You are worrying about the language heard by a well travelled and experienced person of twenty-eight, but you don't care what comes to the ears of a sheltered fifteen year old—

> JENNY *points dramatically at* BERNIE. BERNIE *blushes to the tips of his ears.*

BERNIE: Sixteen come January, Miss.

RUFUS: [*sanctimoniously*] I hope you men do keep a close watch on your tongues when the boy is with you.

> JENNY *seizes her advantage.*

JENNY: So far as I am concerned, Mr Torrent, I have never heard anything said in my presence that might not have been said by a gentleman... a gentleman under stress, sometimes... but always a gentleman.

> RUFUS *has to turn away to hide his involuntary grin—she has turned it neatly.*

JOCK: Oh, lassie—lassie...

JENNY: Mr MacDonald—you've been kind. You're good enough at your own work to know that mine, too, is well enough in its way. Why do you object to me?

JOCK: Well—a fair question deserves a fair reply. I don't object to you meself, lassie. You're a good worker and a pleasant speaker, and I suppose I could get used to the sight of a bit of petticoat going up the stairs every day. But if the others are unhappy about you—and if Mr Torrent's not easy in his mind about getting those new men I need so badly—[*Lamely*] well, I've got to think of what's best for everyone, don't I?

> CHRISTY *looks at* JOCK *with scorn.* BERNIE *is looking at* JENNY.

CHRISTY: [*to* JOCK] A bit of petticoat—

JENNY: And you, Mr Christy—why do you wish to see me gone?

CHRISTY: Well, I—[*Produces his masterpiece*] Because a woman's place is in the home!

JENNY: So, when I am put out of my work here, Mr Christy, will you take me into your home?

CHRISTY: I'm a bachelor!

JENNY: A very good reason for employing me in your home. I should manage it better than many of your home-bred women. Teaching a woman to do her work well in an office is not going to stop her doing it well in the house. On the contrary—

RUFUS: I think this discussion is becoming pointless—

Obviously RUFUS *wants to end it, because* JENNY *has made some points. He walks into his office. He sits at his desk, takes up proofs... it is obvious from his attitude that the dismissal of* JENNY *hasn't gone the way he thought it would. In the outer office,* JOCK, CHRISTY, BERNIE *shuffle.*

JOCK: There's work waiting...

They start out.

Look lass, I'm sorry, but it's not the proper station of life to which the Lord's called you, see. It's not your fault.

They go out, BERNIE *looking back,* JENNY *opens her desk and begins to take out some personal belongings, including a lace handkerchief.* RUFUS *comes from his office,* JENNY *is over at the hat-stand taking her hat off the hook when* RUFUS *comes out of the inner office.* JENNY *is near to tears, but defiant.* RUFUS *is a little ashamed. They look at each other.* RUFUS *gets his hat from the hat-stand. He starts out, stops by the desk... he looks at the collection of* JENNY*'s personal belongings... without thinking he picks up a handkerchief... sniffs the perfume... realises what he is doing and drops it back.* JENNY *seen, watching him.*

RUFUS: I am going out, Miss Milford—

He turns back.

I am sorry, Miss Milford.

JENNY: When I began here, Mr Torrent, they told me you were a hard man—hard but just. I see they were mistaken.

RUFUS: I suppose I do seem unjust to you. As for my hardness, I am sorry for it. But I set myself a task here—and hardness is unavoidable.

JENNY: Oh, I don't think you're hard, Mr Torrent! I think you're rather soft. Well, it is soft to get rid of someone who can be an asset to your business... and you know I can be... because you haven't the strength to be different. It's rather sad.

RUFUS: [*lividly*] I do as I see fit!

JENNY: They said that, too. 'There'll be women working everywhere in Koolgalla soon,' they said—'now that Rufus Torrent has shown the way.' Oh, most of them didn't approve of the idea but they couldn't help—admiring. None of them would have had the courage to engage a woman to work for them. [*Comfortingly*] I expect it will be quite a relief to them that you hadn't, either.

> RUFUS *looks at her. He appraises her move. He is moved to unwilling admiration.*

RUFUS: Miss Milford, you may stay. I would refuse to accept your resignation if you offered it. I will be back in an hour. When I return, I expect to find the advertisements listed, the page make-ups ready for my initialling, and the Council Meeting notes typed up...

JENNY: [*controlling her triumph she says obediently*] Yes, Mr Torrent.

> RUFUS *picks up a type-written page from her desk.*

RUFUS: Miss Milford—you have an unfortunate tendency in otherwise excellent spelling to refuse to recognise that 'E I' generally follows 'C'. Watch that.

> JENNY *nods obediently.*

JENNY: Yes, Mr Torrent.

> *At the door* RUFUS *turns back.*

RUFUS: I hope you realise that I saw the trap that you set for me. No doubt you feel you have achieved a victory. No doubt you have. But since you have chosen to un-sex yourself, do not expect any tolerance for feminine weaknesses. [*A warning*] One mistake, Miss Milford!... I will be back at two o'clock.

> RUFUS *goes out.* JENNY *expresses her delight by putting her belongings back in the desk drawer, hanging her hat back on its peg, dipping a curtsy to the hat stand.* MANSON *comes in*

ACT ONE

as JENNY *is having her little triumphal play. He waits till she sweeps out of the curtsy.*

MANSON: Does the King of Ireland make you bow to his hat-stand, Miss Milford?

    JENNY *is angry at being caught.*

That was a very pretty gesture. What was it for?

JENNY: [*going to her typewriter*] Since there can be no reasonable explanation, Mr Manson, I'll attempt none. Mr Torrent has just gone out.

MANSON: I heard him. I was in the printing room, looking at some proofs... something to do with a bit of a scheme of mine. I don't believe in putting all my eggs in one basket... Where's Ben?

JENNY: [*always very terse with* MANSON] Mr Ben Torrent has not come in yet.

MANSON: Where can I find him?

JENNY: I really don't know, Mr Manson, he may be in Court or—

MANSON: Anywhere... places a lady can't mention.

    JENNY *looks at him coolly.*

I like Ben. I'd like a boy like Ben. [*A deep anger*] Hell, I deserve a boy like Ben...

    JENNY *begins to type.*

Do you like Ben, Miss Milford?

JENNY: I enjoy working here, Mr Manson, with all the staff—

MANSON: Even Rufus Torrent, the King of Ireland.

    JENNY *catches her nail in the keys. She sucks her finger briefly and angrily.*

A bit jumpy today, Miss Milford... ? When Ben comes in, tell him I'll give him a good lunch at the Travellers' Arms... Bubbly in the middle of the day... Y'know something, Miss Milford... ?

    JENNY *looks up to him.*

Twenty-five years, I couldn't've imagined bubbly at all... dirt poor I was... then it was pay dirt. All dirt, though—

    MANSON *starts out, swings back.*

I know you don't like me but I like you. I wouldn't allow a woman of mine to work like a man—but it must take guts. Don't forget to tell Ben I asked him.

> BERNIE *passes* MANSON *in the doorway.* BERNIE *is carrying some proofs.* MANSON *is aware of* BERNIE'S *look at* JENNY. *A great deal of* MANSON'S *success has come from catching people off guard and he never loses an opportunity—not even with* BERNIE.

Don't go turning the boy's head now, Miss Milford—

> *He goes.*

BERNIE: I suppose you think a man showed up in a very poor light, Miss Milford—not taking your part.
JENNY: [*glancing through proofs*] What man… ?
BERNIE: Why—me, Miss Milford!
JENNY: You!

> *She has an impulse to laugh. Then, with his eyes on her, her genuine kindliness prevents this.*

Of course—you.
BERNIE: I've been worrying about not speaking out.
JENNY: That's happened to most of us—not speaking out about something, and then being sorry for it. But there always comes another chance.
BERNIE: Not to speak out for—you.
JENNY: For something more than me next time. But thank you.

> BEN *is heard downstairs, calling 'Jenny'… He comes in.*

BEN: What's all this nonsense about deputations and resignations? You're not to go away. I don't want you to go away!

> JENNY *looks at him. She is aggravated by his peremptory manner. But she is charming to* BERNIE.

JENNY: I'll read this immediately, Bernie—it is all right to call you 'Bernie'?
BERNIE: [*overwhelmed*] Oh, yes, Miss Milford!

> *He exits, very happy.* JENNY *goes back to desk, starts skimming through proofs. She can't contain her annoyance with* BEN.

JENNY: I don't think you should call me by my Christian name, Mr Torrent. It doesn't look well. I have had quite enough trouble in this office without being suspected of undue familiarity—with my employer's son!
BEN: [*laughing*] You sound like a subscription library... [*Posturing*] Sir, I may be but a poor working girl, but my honour means as much to me as to the finest lady in the land!

    JENNY *has to laugh.*

Anyway, you can be free with first names to Bernie.
JENNY: That is rather a different matter...

    She continues to mark the proof. BEN *props against the filing cabinet, looks at her.*

BEN: Why don't you like me, Jenny?
JENNY: I don't dislike you, Ben—
BEN: First name at last!
JENNY: [*crossly*] Oh, since you won't maintain a proper discipline, don't expect me to maintain it for you! I don't dislike you. Everybody likes you. But you're so very, very—[*Hesitates for word.*]
BEN: Is 'spoiled' the word you're looking for?
JENNY: I didn't mean to be rude—

    BEN *begins to play with the blocks, building a house of them on top of the filing cabinet as he talks.*

BEN: I'm Ben Torrent—good position, good prospects, tolerable looks—oh, don't prim up your mouth, Jenny! I inherited my looks from my father, as I inherited everything else—except my lack of private enterprise and public spirit. That's fortunate Koolgalla couldn't stand two public-spirited Torrents. [*Positive*] You're not leaving. I won't have it.
JENNY: That has already been decided—between your father and me. Mr Torrent saw my side of the situation.
BEN: Presented with a certain feminine subtlety?
JENNY: I hope you don't think I cried into my handkerchief—or fluttered my eyelashes?
BEN: Would I suspect you of such cheap tricks? But you're not such a fool that you wouldn't use all your capabilities. You're an

independent woman—not an imitation man... ! And clever women have the advantage, every time.

    BEN *comes close to her.*

You know that's true, don't you, Jenny?

JENNY: Well, Mister—Ben. If I wished to catch a mouse, I wouldn't consider it a proof of independence that I hit it on the head with a hammer... not while there are mousetraps and cheese for the purpose.

    She goes out with the proof. BEN *sits on desk, laughing. He picks up the handkerchief she has left behind and smells the perfume.*

ACT ONE CURTAIN

ACT TWO

SCENE ONE

Three weeks later. A meeting of directors is in progress at the office. A big table has been moved in for the occasion, jamming the room. RUFUS *sits easily at the head of it, with* JENNY *at her desk behind him and to one side. The other five directors and shareholders sit on either side.*

MANSON, *big and dominant;* SQUIRES, *a shrewd rather mean little man;* TWIMPLE, *pleasant but ineffectual, very much in awe of both* RUFUS *and* MANSON; *the* STUWELLS, *father and son, father the leading storekeeper—rather pompous. With his bored son,* CHARLIE. *At the opposite end of the table to* RUFUS *sits* BEN, *coiled like a spring, tense, watching* KINGSLEY MYERS *who has been addressing the meeting.* KINGSLEY *hasn't much hope, but he's still trying.*

KINGSLEY: … and as you gentleman can see from these plans [*Bending over plans laid out on table*] it would be possible to pipe streams of water from the main source and to divert them, where necessary, over land in cultivation. This portion here, which would flow across Simmerton's Flat—

MANSON: Happens that's the richest gold bearing ground on the fields, Kingsley—but then so's the rest of the land you're after. And you want to plant—cabbages—on it!

They all laugh.

STUWELL SNR: One of the richest fields in that country, that was—
BEN: Was.
STUWELL SNR: Is. Plenty of it there still. Isn't that so, Charlie. Speak up son.
CHARLIE: Loads.

He resumes his covert studying of JENNY, *to which she replies with a chilling look and tucks her ankles well under her skirt.*

TWIMPLE: Now if we could combine both enterprises satisfactorily…

He looks hopefully at KINGSLEY, *for* MR TWIMPLE *likes things to go pleasantly.*

KINGSLEY: [*definitely*] Impossible, Mr Twimple. You can't plant gold gentlemen. Once it's gone, the land lies dead and useless. But plant and water and harvest—put your work back into the land, and the land is grateful for it.

SQUIRES: The land may be—er—grateful Mr Myers, but what about the people to work it.

MANSON *smacks his hand approvingly on the desk.*

There are farms all over the country crying out for men—and they can't get them! And it's not money—the wages being offered are higher than ever before—but still the men stay on the fields. Not only the farms going short-handed, either—ships, stores—that is so, isn't it Mr Stuwell?

STUWELL SNR: There's a notice in my left window at this moment—'Man wanted!'—been there for months. And what did we get in all that time… ?

CHARLIE: [*unexpectedly animated*] Little fellow in a lavender striped shirt—worked for us for a week, then took his pay out in tools, and joined up with Mike O'Brien in French's Gully.

STUWELL SNR: That's right son—speak up. And Charlie here's been doing every hands turn about the place ever since.

CHARLIE: Damned dullish…

MANSON: There's your point, Myers. I've got nothing against new ideas—I like to see things go ahead. There's always something in progress for the go-ahead man, and I like a fight of any kind—apart from the money to win. But Squires's got you—who's going to do the work? Some of Torrent's Irish pixies, maybe?

He laughs, followed by the others. RUFUS *looks at a portion of the wall through* MANSON*'s head.*

KINGSLEY: [*after a swift and bitter glance at* RUFUS] I see that Mr Torrent has already discussed his objections with you gentlemen. He pointed out to me earlier that he did not believe that the town will give up their chance of easy fortune for such a scheme as this.

RUFUS *looks up quickly about to deny this, for it has been pure chance. But seeing* BEN*'s accusing look he stiffens and remains silent.*

I still think that people can see their way into the future better than you believe. But to do so, they would have to know the alternatives. I had hoped that the *Argus* would support this scheme. It seems I was foolish. But can't you at least state the details—be absolutely impartial, you prepare the statement from my technical details...

He looks at them all... Their stonewall faces halt him.

[*Briefly, directly to* RUFUS] Shall I leave these?

Gestures to diagrams.

RUFUS: [*looking in his turn at the others. Then, with an understanding of* KINGSLEY*'s feelings*] Take them Kingsley. We'll send for them—if we want them.

KINGSLEY *picks up the diagrams. Looks at* BEN *for a moment, then turns on his heels and walks out.* BEN *half rises as though to follow him. Then he swings to* RUFUS.

BEN: You could have given him that at least! You could have abbreviated a church notice or cut out a social note and given him one day's space to speak. Or since we're [*Contemptuously*] business men here, let him buy it and have his say!

RUFUS: No. [*First to* BEN *then to the others*] No. The price of the *Argus* is two pence. For that you get the whole paper. But outside of advertising—and Kingsley's scheme is not that—you can't buy one line of the *Argus*—and never will, while I'm editor here.

STUWELL SNR: You wouldn't call a newspaper a business really—not like a store now. It's more of an interest—eh?

Looks at CHARLIE *who seems far from taking an interest in anything.* STUWELL *gives in, on a pensive 'Yes...'*

RUFUS: Right, Ben—we're business men here. But it happens that in our business we deal in peculiar commodities—events after they happen, and plans before they are realised. [*Swinging on them*] Make no mistake gentlemen—whether you think it right or wrong, the idea of this project must be faced by you sometime. Kingsley is not a single fanatic—whether or not the gold is running out in

Koolgalla, it has run out in other places—and men are looking for new ways to live. Some time, I tell you, you will have to make up your minds—for or against. You can't just sit by and let him state his case—you—we—must either attack it bitterly as a dangerous and useless project, or give it our support as necessary life blood to a dying town!

TWIMPLE: [*worried*] But would you say a crisis was approaching, Mr Torrent. I must say that I haven't noticed any falling off in my legal—er—commitments...

STUWELL SNR: Nothing wrong with my store—and my store was built on the diggings trade. [*Heartening himself*] Oh, imagine the gold running out in Koolgalla!

BEN: Imagine it! Haven't you seen the empty stores in Cresswell, Mr Stuwell?—shovels and billies and panning dishes still shiny under the dust on the wrappings... the broken office windows in Dalton's Crossing, Mr Twimple, the courthouse falling down...

> STUWELL *and* TWIMPLE *look a little aghast. Could there be anything in it?* CHARLIE *bites a nail in vague worry.* MANSON *frowns.* MANSON *rides in.*

MANSON: [*strong*] And what if it does happen here? We're not tied hand and foot are we? The gold can run out in the ground, but gold is where you find it. We found it before, didn't we? Let it go then. We're not finished if it does.

BEN: There'll be plenty of people in Koolgalla who will be—if the gold goes, and there's nothing else.

MANSON: You won't be one of 'em Ben... your father's seen to that.

BEN: Do you think that would be the only thing that would count with me?

MANSON: No. But it's the first thing—it has to be. [*This is* MANSON*'s declaration*] You can't give anything away, Ben, until you've got enough for yourself—whether it's money, land or dreams.

> *Unawares* JENNY*'s lip curls in contempt.*

Yes Miss Jenny, I understand dreams too! [*To* BEN] I'm not so old that I've forgotten what ideas a young man has. But it's a hard world Ben. When you're young, you think you can make it a heaven on earth—all for yourself and enough for everyone else... but you get

ACT TWO

that knocked out of you! Two hands and a brain, that's what God gives to everyone, for himself. And you've got to take what you can with them!

Suddenly he leans across and takes BEN's *hand, holding it flat, comparing it with his own.*

I've worked hard for what I've got. I froze in Canada, got the yellow fever in Brazil, dysentery in India—and I came to Koolgalla, broke, Ben—hungry—broke. Then I took a parcel out of Simmerton's Flat... But I'd earned it already! You can't make life easy—not for yourself or anyone else, Ben. All you do that way is breed a race of weaklings, expecting to be saved. There's plenty in the world to be taken for the fighting—and any man who doesn't fight, doesn't deserve it. [*Challenging*] You've made your way in the world, Torrent—have you anything to add to that?

RUFUS: Nothing, Mr Manson—you're so eloquent that you might be Irish!

MANSON: I haven't got a son to advise, Torrent. If I had I'd say this. 'Australia's a big country. And it's yours for the taking!' When we're finished here, we've only emptied one barrel—so throw it away, Ben. Throw it away and open the next!

His magnetism holds BEN, *who feels himself swayed though against his own convictions.*

You're not the kind of boy who's meant to scratch the earth for cabbages!

BEN: I wish I could be as eloquent as my father. I wish I could put my arguments as well as Mr Manson. Gentlemen I beg of you. Forget that I'm young—overlook that the mechanics of this plan are meaningless to me. Let me urge you to give this thing a chance. Don't pass up the future for the sake of the present that is nearly past. Don't pass up the glorious—impossible—realisable chance.

RUFUS: [*wanting to save him*] Ben...

BEN: [*wearily and emptily*] I know, Father. I sound like a fool. Excuse me gentlemen.

At the door he turns back, bitterly.

Oh, damn all you old—cautious—safe men. You make the world unsure!

> BEN *starts out. Forgetting where she is,* JENNY *stands up, her notebook falling to the floor.* BEN *looks, goes out.* MANSON *picks up* JENNY'*s notebook and restores it to her elaborately. He looks over his shoulder at* RUFUS.

MANSON: [*baiting* RUFUS] Be careful Torrent—or you'll lose him.
TWIMPLE: He has generous sympathies, Mr Torrent.

> MANSON *goes on wanting to irritate* RUFUS.

MANSON: I wouldn't let it worry you that he gets crazy ideas about the world. All kids do. You might even've had some yourself once—but you've learned to knuckle down. Nothing like going short of bread to make a man learn what side it's buttered on when he gets it!

RUFUS: [*exploding*] I've learned many things myself, Mr Manson—but by thunder, I've never learned to lick the butter off my bread—and my son will never learn it either. You're my directors, your money is in my paper—and I bow to that—a certain way. I've listened to you—now you listen to me! I've told you that one day you'll have to make up your minds about this plan. Why not make them up now—and favourably. [*Back to* MANSON] For it's true—and you know it—that while the gold supply is continuing, it is running thinner. People who once made a good and easy living are now scraping the earth for their loaves of bread—and the men with gold in their pockets from Simmerton's Flat get fewer and fewer, Mr Manson. There are no more fortunes to be made except by the people who sell the loaves of bread and the God-given earth the people scrape. [*To* STUWELL] And not for long—think of that! For who makes money in a dead town?

MANSON: I've told you—move on.

RUFUS: [*he is concentrating on* STUWELL *and* TWIMPLE *knowing that* MANSON *will not come his way*] Somewhere you have to stay. And in that place you have to build as well as take. Shall this be our stopping place, gentlemen? Shall we harness the river, and make the town grow, and show them that the *Argus* moves ahead of the times?

> *It is a good effort and* TWIMPLE *and* STUWELL *are swaying.*

STUWELL SNR: It'd take money…
TWIMPLE: You've shown logic there, Mr Torrent…

ACT TWO

SQUIRES: [*as* RUFUS *looks at him*] I would like to hear what Mr Manson thinks about it.

MANSON: [*standing at window, looking down on town*] What do I think? I think Torrent makes up his mind very suddenly—unless it was made up already. Maybe he's got other interests he's not telling us.

SQUIRES: It is a rapid decision, Mr Torrent. I don't want to pry, but if this scheme of Mr Myers might be accepted by the Lands Department... I suppose it could be—certain property investments might become very valuable. [*Shrewdly*] Yours, perhaps...? So why not ours—if you have the information to share...

RUFUS: Mr Squires, there is a rodent not yet registered in the catalogue of Australian animals—the lavatory rat—

He bows formally to JENNY.

—Excuse the term, Miss Milford.

JENNY *indicates 'pardon granted'*.

STUWELL SNR: I hope no-one's calling no-one a rat...

MANSON *picks up his hat*.

MANSON: Maybe Torrent wants to impress his son [*He looks at* JENNY.] or someone—that he's still young and adventurous. Nothing like youth to wake up the last of a man's middle years. Well, I don't fancy paying for it with my money...

The finger stabs at them all.

... and don't forget—that's what it'll come to in the end... rates, taxes, levies, loans—money... to pay for Torrent's public spirit. Your money. Not mine. Coming, Squires?

SQUIRES *joins him, bows to* JENNY.

SQUIRES: Under the present circumstances, I think further discussion would be quite out of order.

There's a stir among the STUWELLs, TWIMPLE... *they don't want to be left alone with* RUFUS.

TWIMPLE: [*edging his way out*] I do feel that we might—at a later date, perhaps...

MANSON: Don't carry your head too high, Torrent… easier to bring it down.

He and SQUIRES *go after bowing to* JENNY.

STUWELL SNR: Well, everyone's got a right to their own opinion, haven't they? [*To* CHARLIE] That's right, isn't it? Speak up, son…

CHARLIE: Yes. My opinion is that you're all bloody silly not to jump at Myers' idea. Of course it'll work. Oh, come on, Dad—I want a drink!

CHARLIE STUWELL gives JENNY an outrageous wink—he gets a big smile. He goes. STUWELL SNR *follows, saying feebly…*

STUWELL SNR: That's right, Charlie—speak up, son…

JENNY, RUFUS *left alone.*

RUFUS: Who could have expected that from Stuwell Junior?

RUFUS *sits on the edge of the big table.*

God, I'm so tired…

JENNY *looks at him. Then she goes into his office, and begins to rummage through desk drawers.*

I thought I could sway them. But the moment Manson said 'money', they followed him like frightened sheep.

JENNY *offers him whisky.*

And how did you know that was there?

JENNY: A good secretary knows where every essential is to be found.

RUFUS *drinks the stiff whisky she pours him.*

You know that Kingsley's dream can come true…

RUFUS: [*savagely*] How do I know that? How do I know if a thing is right until I see it before my eyes? It's precious few of us, young lady, who can see the realities of dreams. No, it was no burning conviction—it was my destiny—my stupid Irish temper and my damned Irish pride.

From this point on he forgets who she is, realising only that he is tired, discouraged, desperately in need of an outlet for all the emotion he bottles up, and she is sympathetic.

ACT TWO 35

I've worked for years to conquer them—to be cool and wise and responsible—an English gentleman in fact—and they trap me still! And suddenly there I am risking myself like a gambler on a chance card, fighting a fight that should be no fight of mine.

As though answering an unspoken need, JENNY *comes softly to the chair next to* RUFUS *and sits in it, her chin on her hands, looking at him obliquely across the table.*

JENNY: Must your destiny be only pride and anger?

RUFUS: It's the destiny of any Dubliner—any poverty stricken, broken footed, torn trousered, Dubliner. Be proud and angry enough to cut your way out—or else fumble and go under—fumble with your person, fumble with your girl, fumble with your God—and so be trapped! I was not to be trapped!

JENNY: What did you do?

RUFUS: Denied my world—parents, friends, girls—even my God. So I denied and defied all. And where has it led me... ?

JENNY: Here, to Koolgalla—free of the past and with your soul your own?

RUFUS: Is any Irishman free of his past? You don't understand. Being Irish isn't a nationality—it's a disease!

JENNY gives him another whisky, and she laughs.

[*Lightly*] I can see you don't approve of us.

JENNY: Oh, you have charm—and the bright courage on the brink of the grave that makes men love you... Yes, and you've made your wit part of this country, so that in all their heroics there will always be a taste of wryness, and the cream of their jest will always be sour! But you hug your hurt pride to your heart and pride yourself on your ability to live alone. I tell you, to live alone is nothing! Anybody can do it! But to live with the world—not to perish, but to work for it—not to weep for it, but to change it—that makes a man—or a woman! And if everything fails—love and religion, faith, hope and charity are proven lies, there is still something left that can make us go on!

She is almost hurling the words at him... suddenly she breaks and her own doubts and bewilderment catch up on her. She falters and in a sudden collapse which is almost childish says...

But I don't know what it is, or how to find it.

RUFUS: [*tenderly*] You don't need to search, Jenny. You have it in your heart. And what do you know of battles?

JENNY: I am as much a soldier as any of your Irish heroes. I fight for the things I believe in… and it's a desolate thing sometimes to seem to be the one woman alone on such a new battleground.

RUFUS: You chose it, you—NEW—woman!

JENNY: And proud of it! If you have to fight then always choose your battleground! That is only common sense!

RUFUS: And you know what you fight for?

JENNY: Yes.

This is straight in the eye. They are very close. Slowly he puts out a hand and touches her lightly on the shoulder, as though acknowledging her equality.

RUFUS: I believe you do—and will achieve it.

JENNY: [*eagerly*] That is why I felt so much for Ben today…

RUFUS *begins to chill.*

That was his battleground… and you mustn't let him feel he was driven from it in defeat. He will be such a fine man. But he needs encouragement, inspiration…

RUFUS *has turned away from her. Very deliberately he moves to the hat rack, takes down hat, puts it on.*

RUFUS: I think my son has reached the age when he must learn to make his own decisions, Miss Milford. If he does need—er inspiration, Miss Milford, I am confident that it can be supplied by his fiancée… the proper person, Miss Milford, to give solace and comfort…

It is dawning on JENNY *that this is a rebuke administered to her. She is hurt and angry.* RUFUS *turns at the door.*

When you have typed the editorial, Miss Milford, you may go. And please remember that 'E I' still follows 'C' as a general rule.

He goes out on the angry JENNY. JENNY *tosses off the last of his whisky—and chokes on it.*

ACT TWO   37

SCENE TWO

An hour later, the same evening. JENNY *is sitting at the small table, a block in her hand that she has taken from the box, her thoughts far from pleasant.* CHRISTY *pops through the centre entrance.*

CHRISTY: Editorial ready?

Startled, the block flies out of JENNY'*s hand on to the floor.*

JENNY: Oh—you startled me, Christy.
CHRISTY: 'Course, I move like a cat—learned it from the blacks, y'know... lived with 'em for years when I...

With a sudden apprehensive glance at the inner office door, he jerks an enquiring thumb.

In?
JENNY: Out.
CHRISTY: [*relieved, trots over to her*] Oh. Now where was I? Oh, yes, you were asking about me living with the blacks. Well, it was when I was shipwrecked when the Lustre Bell struck off the Cape. Would've died but for them blacks... When I caught up with the white men again and I left, they cried—the whole tribe just cried!
JENNY: I believe they would.
CHRISTY: And then there was this other time
JOCK: [*bellowing from downstairs*] Christy!
CHRISTY: [*yelling from the stairs*] What?
JOCK: The editorial, you numbskull!
CHRISTY: Coming. [*Chuckles, unregenerate*] Knew there was something on me mind. Have you got the editorial ready?
JENNY: Mr Torrent's done it, Christy, but I haven't quite finished typing it.

She stands up to move to typewriter.

I'll do it now.
CHRISTY: [*gleefully*] Don't worry yourself. You been busy this afternoon with the [*Contemptuously*] Directors' Meeting?
JENNY: Rather busy...

CHRISTY: Newspapers never had 'directors' when I worked on 'em first. Just a damn nuisance! [*Cunningly*] Did I hear the Old Man bellowing!

JENNY: [*demurely*] How could you, Christy—all the way downstairs.

CHRISTY: No need to tell anyone, when his lordship lets his lungs out for an airing. Was it Manson got his goat? He's got the devil's own temper when it's up.

JENNY: [*determinedly*] Christy, you must go down now and tell Mr MacDonald that I'll bring this editorial down in a few minutes…

She gives CHRISTY *a gentle push in the direction of the door.*

CHRISTY: [*going slowly, still chuckling*] Oh, he's got a fine temper alright! By God, if he finds out that young Ben is over at the Royal, filling himself up with whisky, there'll be such a—

He is almost out by this, but JENNY *pulls him back with such force and abruptness that* CHRISTY *is left gasping.*

JENNY: What did you say?

CHRISTY [*bemused*] What did I say?

JENNY: [*almost shaking him*] About Ben!

CHRISTY: Only that he's over at the Royal, filling himself up, with whisky—[*A private grievance*] and us slaving here!

JENNY: Christy, what will I do? Should I go over there and get him out?

CHRISTY: [*appalled*] By Grundy, Jenny, you can't do that. Some of them drinkers are pretty far gone!

JENNY: [*contemptuously*] I won't be shocked.

CHRISTY: No… but, by God, they will be! You can't do that, Jenny…

JENNY *has moved across the window and is looking out.*

JENNY: But we can't just leave him there—in that place!

CHRISTY: Oh, the Royal's not a bad pub.

Looks around as BEN *comes in, rather drunk and defiant. He jerks his head at* CHRISTY *in direction of stairs and* CHRISTY, *glad to escape, goes.*

[*As he vanishes*] Ten minutes you said…

BEN: Looking for someone, Jenny?

JENNY: [*whirling around*] Ben! What have you been doing?

ACT TWO

BEN: Didn't anyone in Koolgalla find time to tell you—or were they all hurrying to tell Father? I've been drinking.
JENNY: Oh, I know that. [*Scornfully*] I can see it.
BEN: Yes, I'm afraid I don't do it very well. But I'll improve with practice.
JENNY: Stop talking like that.

She brushes past him and goes to typewriter, sits down and begins to type on sheet in machine, banging through BEN's *speeches.*

It sounds so childish!
BEN: Isn't that in keeping with my previous speech—the one I made today—or didn't make today—the stupid bumbling one I made, while they all sat round and grinned magnanimously. [*Shouting*] Must you rattle that infernal machine?
JENNY: [*still going*] I have two more paragraphs of the editorial—
BEN: Oh, yes, my dear father's editorial! And what has my father to say to the public today?
JENNY: Advocating better means of communication—

BEN *drags some crumpled sheets of copy paper out of his pocket, looks at it morosely, and stuffs it back.* JENNY's *eyes follow the sheets.*

BEN: Better means of communication. By all means—let us communicate with one another—freely and pleasantly, and without attempting to face vexatious problems which can only bring us discomfort and ridicule. [*Sincerely*] Poor King, I told him I'd do my best and I failed him, didn't I?
JENNY: No, you didn't, Ben… and King would be the last to think that. You tried to say something. At least, you tried!
BEN: And with such wonderful effect. I suppose my father had everyone smoothed and smiling in five minutes!
JENNY: He didn't! He carried on where you left off. He was wonderful! He defended you… !

This is the wrong thing to say. The whisky in BEN *rises.*

BEN: I can defend myself. And when he defended Kingsley's plans—he did it better than I did, didn't he, Jenny?

JENNY: Ben, I was so proud of you when you spoke—
BEN: [*flatly*] But my father did it so much better.
JENNY: He's had so much more experience with these things—
BEN: He's so much cleverer, so much cooler, so much more dominating. Jenny, I have lived in my father's shadow all my life. Oh, don't think I haven't loved him, like everyone else, I've fallen under the spell. I tell you, Jenny, I have come to believe that if I ever truly loved a woman, my father—if it occurred to him—could win her from me like that!

> *He snaps his finger.*

Does that shock you, Jenny?
JENNY: [*slowly*] If you ever truly loved a woman… What about Gwynne?
BEN: [*arrested*] Gwynne…

> *He turns away to stare out the window.*

Gwynne. Oh, I know she's a sweet person and a good woman and—
JENNY: And she is to be your wife.
BEN: [*with a dignified candour which infuriates* JENNY] I know that, Jenny—and however weak you may think me, I am not weak enough to go back on the word I've given.

> *He looks for approbation and is shocked when* JENNY *snarls at him.*

JENNY: That's a very generous gesture, Ben! Oh, why does every man consider himself such a prize that it becomes the highest pledge of gentlemanly honour to marry the woman… yes, marry her, and patronise and belittle her for the rest of your lives together, complimenting yourselves for your divine condescension.

> BEN *opens his mouth to speak.*

No, don't deny it! Do you wonder, then, that we—the ones you call in your contempt, the New Women—that we fight for our right to an independent wage, an independent mind, an independent life… [*Advancing on* BEN] and, one day, my fine friend, we will be condescending if we marry YOU!
BEN: [*laughing but sobered by her vehemence*] Jenny for Governor!

ACT TWO 41

JENNY: [*rather flattened*] You can laugh, Ben. But you have no right to speak of Gwynne like that.

BEN: [*haughtily*] When I marry her, I will consider it my duty to devote myself to her happiness.

JENNY: Duty... you, who cannot take this afternoon's set-back without flying to alcohol! You, who are much too self-indulgent, not to gratify your own desires. If you—[*She hesitates*] If you should meet a woman who meant more to you, would you deny yourself—for Gwynne!

After a moment, BEN *turns away from her eyes.*

What would she suffer then? No—better to be brave now and let her turn to someone who does love her—someone like Kingsley—

BEN: Kingsley appears to have the knack of inspiring—confidence.

JENNY: [*flushing with fury*] Oh, you men—you talk glibly of women's preoccupation with love-making, and yet you cannot bear another man praised without accusing her in your thoughts! Oh, I'm so tired of men!

Flounces back to her desk, gives typescript to BEN.

If you will take this down to Mr MacDonald, I can go home.

BEN *takes the papers... then he turns back.*

BEN: [*sincerely*] I'm sorry, Jenny. I'm weak and I hate it.

JENNY: You are weak Ben. And you're denying your own talent because you're afraid of it, just as your father denies the rebellion of his heart. You're a journalist, Ben—you could write—you could explain to everyone in Koolgalla just what Kingsley's dream can mean. You could do it, Ben.

BEN *turns his back on her, walks slowly to her desk drops typescript on it, deep in his sense of defeat.*

BEN: I can't. I tried today. There it is. But it isn't any use.

She comes quickly across the room, picks up typescript and begins to read it. BEN *can't help watching her reaction as she flicks over the first page.*

JENNY: [*delighted*] It's good, Ben—it's good!
BEN: I didn't think it was too bad, myself.

She is reading on.

Of course, most of that [*Indicates pages*] is Kingsley talking.

JENNY: But it isn't. Kingsley talks for himself—and while he understands it, others may not. But this, this is written so that everyone will be able to understand. Everyone will see why it's so important that we should beat our picks into plough shares.

BEN: Good, Jenny, that's good—we ought to put that in… before we throw it in the wastepaper basket.

JENNY: [*horrified*] You don't mean you're not going to do anything with this?

BEN: What can I do?

JENNY: Print it! The space is waiting…

BEN: Print something in Rufus Torrent's paper without his permission, and something with which he disagrees? Father would go stark raving mad if I did!

JENNY: [*shortly*] Let him! Anyway, he doesn't disagree, he said as much as this himself, this afternoon.

BEN: Then for the sake of all our necks, let us leave him to write it himself, too. Toss it in the wastepaper basket, Jenny—or keep it as a souvenir of Ben Torrent's first and last rebellion.

He starts for door.

And now I'm going to resume my practice—at the private bar of the Royal.

Turns back.

Don't leave that stuff lying around.

JENNY: Oh, Ben! [*Fiercely*] Ben—are you afraid of your father?

BEN: [*as he exits*] Yes.

He goes.

JENNY: [*forgetting her dignity and yelling after him*] And when they carry you out, I'll tell them to deliver you to Gwynne. It's the gentlemanly thing, isn't it, to allow the lady to unlace your boots and be sick in her lap?

She is screwing up the pages nervously when BERNIE *comes in.*

BERNIE: Did you call, Miss Milford? Is it ready?

ACT TWO 43

JENNY: [*snapping*] What…? I'm sorry, Bernie. I'm… I'm out of sorts.
BERNIE: Gee, could I do anything… ?
JENNY: No, thanks, Bernie. I suppose you want the editorial.

Goes to desk and picks it up, she is rather close to tears.

Here you are, Bernie—guaranteed not to set the town on fire…

She stops… she looks at both sets of papers. She gives BERNIE BEN*'s article.*

Take this to Mr MacDonald, Bernie—tell him I'm sorry I kept him waiting but there was a—a last minute change of policy. And Bernie—Have this set double face and bold.
BERNIE: Right.

JENNY *watches as he runs for the stairs.*

ACT TWO CURTAIN

ACT THREE

SCENE ONE

The Argus *office, the following morning. Bright morning light is coming through the windows, and as the curtain goes up,* RUFUS *comes out of the inner office with* JENNY*'s letter in one hand, a copy of the* Argus *in the other. He is standing in the middle of the stage, bellowing…*

RUFUS: MacDonald! MacDonald! [*Then*] Christy! Where the blazing hell is everybody? CHRISTY!!

    A startled CHRISTY *appears round the door.*

So you're here at last! Where is MacDonald? More to the point—where is—where is that—[*He struggles for words.*] Where is Miss Milford?

CHRISTY: 'S only half past eight, Mr Torrent. She don't start work till nine o'clock.

RUFUS: Nine… ! D'you think I'm going to wait for her till nine? Eh?

    CHRISTY *is considering the diplomatic answer.*

Do you know where she lives?

CHRISTY [*all knowledgeable*] Yes…

RUFUS: Then get her here immediately!

CHRISTY: But—she might still be in bed!

BEN: [*meaning it*] Then drag her out of it!

CHRISTY: [*horrified*] Who—me? By God, I don't. Who—me? Me—

    JENNY *has appeared in the doorway. Although quaking inwardly, she is neatly dressed and looks calm and fresh.*

JENNY: [*sweetly*] It's quite alright, Christy. I am here.

    She comes in, hangs her hat carefully below RUFUS*'.*

I came into the office early, it occurred to me that Mr Torrent might wish to see me.

RUFUS: [*choking*] It occurred to you! One mistake. Miss—!

    JENNY *indicates* CHRISTY *with a discreet nod which serves to*

ACT THREE 45

infuriate RUFUS *further.*

Get out!

CHRISTY: [*indignant*] By Grundy, that's no way to speak to me, Mr Torrent. By Grundy...

RUFUS *swings on him and* CHRISTY *retires.*

No—it's no use trying to apologise! I'm not staying here!

As CHRISTY *goes hastily,* JENNY *moves to her desk.*

RUFUS: As for you, madam—have you any explanation for your—unwarranted—impudent, mischievous—interference...

JENNY: [*cool and kind*] Are you quite well, Mr Torrent... Your face is so flushed...

RUFUS, *scarlet by now, throws up a hand in despair.*

After all—there comes a time when we all have to consider our health.

RUFUS: [*starting quietly*] I am not yet so old, nor so decrepit, Miss Milford—that I am likely to collapse from a—quite understandable—annoyance! I am perfectly at ease—[*Bellowing*] PERFECTLY!

Warned by her expression he drops his voice carefully.

I am scarcely perturbed by the knowledge that my paper is ruined, that I am ridiculed, that my son is clay—wet clay, in the hands of a—a...

Facing her straight look he drops the sentence.

Incidentally, this morning—when I saw the 'Argus'—I asked my son to leave my house.

JENNY: [*sincerely*] Poor Ben—I'm so sorry...

RUFUS *walks to desk and looks down on her.*

RUFUS: [*in a quieter voice*] I think it is only right that I should tell you that my son accepted full blame for that statement. He said he had done it alone. But I am not completely a fool, Miss Milford. I could tell from his bewilderment that he had not expected it to appear. However, he did not mean to—give you away.

JENNY: I did not mean to allow him to be blamed, sir. Surely you found my statement—and my resignation—on your desk?

RUFUS: [*nodding*] I found it. A typical piece of feminine heroics—and again disregarding the fact that 'E I' generally follows 'C'.

> JENNY *has to laugh. She realises she has done it again. She starts to take her belongings out of the desk drawer.* RUFUS *throws letter in wastepaper basket. It misses.*

JENNY: I think that clears everyone of any responsibility—except myself. You can publish it as it stands. I believe it covers everything.

RUFUS: Except one thing. You didn't write that editorial—and Ben did.

JENNY: And you should be proud of him! He put into words the problem that everyone in Koolgalla has to face—and the solution to it. Though you publish fifty retractions, Mr Torrent, you can't wipe that article from their thoughts.

RUFUS: I should have known, when I denied my better judgement, and took a woman into this office that we might expect some kind of specious underhand, interfering feminine logic… !

JENNY: … instead of open, honest, manly illogic!

RUFUS: If you were a man, madam, I would know how to deal with your action!

JENNY: If you were a man, Mr Torrent, you'd stand by it!

> RUFUS *gives a fleeting thought to murder.* MANSON *and* SQUIRES *storm in.*

MANSON: So you did it! I should have known when we left yesterday afternoon and you were standing there, raging inside! Just once or twice I thought to myself—is he going to try to ram this down our necks? Don't you know, you stupid Irish paddy, what directors' meetings are for? Or did you think we were giving you our blessings and asking you to sink our money—our money!… My God, it's the damned insolence of it that sticks in my throat—the damned high-and-mighty, go-to-hell insolence of it!

RUFUS: [*coldly*] My secretary is present, Mr Manson.

MANSON: Then let her go somewhere else! I want to talk to you! And you won't want her to hear some of the things I'm going to say.

> JENNY *stands up to go.*

SQUIRES: I'd be discreet, Mr Manson. Things can be misconstrued. I'm

ACT THREE

sure nobody thinks of coming to court cases, but—
MANSON: All right, Torrent, we'll go into your office.
RUFUS: Whatever you have to say, it may be said in front of Miss Milford. She is completely in my confidence.

He waves JENNY *back imperiously and she sits.*

SQUIRES: Well, I think Mr Manson's irritation is understandable, and I must say that when I put money into a newspaper I do expect my opinions to be at least considered. After all we all have to look after our own—
RUFUS: I thought the devil undertook that task.
MANSON: I wonder if I did misjudge you, Torrent. Yesterday, I said things to prickle you... [*He looks at* JENNY.] but I wasn't really thinking about money. I wonder if you are getting something out of this scheme. If you are—so are we!
RUFUS: You accuse me of corruption?
SQUIRES: No—no. You put too harsh a word upon it... a libellous word!
MANSON: I'd put the word on it—if I knew what game you're playing. If it's just your bog-Irish pride that made you do it, then take a tip from me, and eat it! Retract every word of the damned editorial. Say it was a mistake, you were drunk, you were sunstruck—but deny every word you wrote. You did write it, I suppose?
RUFUS: No.

JENNY *is watching him, breathless.*

My son wrote it. And I may say, Mr Manson, I am proud of him. He took those facts that we refused to face and he stuck them in front of the eyes of the people who needed most to know them. He did his duty as a journalist—with honour and skill. And if a few noses should turn up—well, we'll bear it.
MANSON: We'll bear it! By heaven, I won't!
SQUIRES: Fair is fair, Mr Torrent. Every man must protect his interests. We've spent time and money building businesses—developing them. You must understand, Mr Torrent—
MANSON: Understand, hell! I don't want him to understand, so long as he takes orders. And if he doesn't—it's retraction or ruin, Torrent. None of us, not even that fool Twimple, will follow you in this. We'll take out every penny we've put into the 'Argus' and I happen

to know how much you need it for your grand schemes! We'll take it out!

RUFUS: [*the brogue showing*] Take it out, then—in fact, I'll buy you out! And be damned to you all for a pack of money-grabbing, small minded, mean-soured pedlars, and the town—and the paper—well rid of the lot of you.

> MANSON *lowers his head like an angry bull. Then he straightens and faces* RUFUS.

MANSON: Right, my fine gentleman. Now we know where we stand. Let the others do as they like. I know what I'll do. When I said 'ruin' I wasn't playing with words. You want a fight—you'll get it—and if it's possible to ruin you... and I've ruined men before now—I'll do it! By the time I've finished with you, you'll wish you'd stayed digging potatoes—you'll wish you had some in your stewpot. I never give quarter!

RUFUS: I never ask it.

MANSON: Good. Come on, Squires—I'm off to see Twimple. You coming?

SQUIRES: Yes, Mr Manson. But Mr Torrent, might I ask if there is something more to this scheme than might show to the—uninitiated, could we say? Some Government influence at work, some new discovery perhaps? Surely it would be friendly to tip the wink as they say...

MANSON: [*off*] Squires!

RUFUS: Mr Manson is calling for you, Mr Squires.

SQUIRES: Coming, Mr Manson...

> *He scurries off.* RUFUS *begins to laugh. Still laughing, he walks to the window, stands looking down into the street. He has stopped laughing. He is thinking hard.* JENNY *goes to stand on the other side of the window.*

JENNY: Can you buy them all out, Mr Torrent?

RUFUS: [*this is what he has been considering*] No—not all of them.

> *He smiles at her.*

But if I mortgage everything I own, I can buy out Manson and Squires, which will be good riddance, and I can talk the others into staying with me. I'm not an Irishman for nothing, Miss Milford. In a year they'll be complimenting themselves on their foresight and public spirit [*Dryly*] and so will I!

There is a brief tap on the head of the stairs and JOCK MACDONALD, CHRISTY *and a nervous but determined* BERNIE *in the rear, file in, heavy with serious intention.*

JOCK: [*very Scots, with determination*] Ye'll excuse me, Mr Torrent—I know you're having rather a disturbing morning. But I thought—

CHRISTY *pulls his coat.*

All right, all right—WE thought, but the boys asked me to do the talking—

CHRISTY: Then get on with it!

JOCK: It's no use pretending that we don't know that something peculiar's been going on Mr Torrent. There was that editorial. We know you never saw it—

JENNY: [*quickly*] Mr Torrent knows that nobody was to blame for that but me. I left him an explanation with my resignation. You have no need to feel concerned, Mr MacDonald.

JOCK: [*doggedly*] We know you never saw it—we knew it last night. But we printed it—so we're just as much to blame. You've been a fair employer and a good friend, Mr Torrent, despite your little oddities, and we don't want to make any trouble... Well, sir, if anything is going to happen to the lassie here—or to Ben—we might have to down tools. It's only right we stand by them!

RUFUS *speaks with gentle acidity.*

RUFUS: Thank you, gentlemen. I am touched by the faith in my stupidity and tyranny shown by all my staff. Had you had the opportunity to question Mr Manson and Mr Squires, you would have learned that I, too, am 'standing by them'. The 'Koolgalla Argus' needs no scapegoats!

General relief CHRISTY *guffaws with satisfaction.*

CHRISTY: I could've told you—I could've told you—!

JOCK: [*who does not approve of drama in the office*] Then why didn't you, you perishing genius, and save everybody's time! Now that's settled satisfactorily, Mr Torrent, we'll be getting back to work.

Jerks his head toward door and they start out.

JENNY: Wait—please.

They turn back.

You know I can't say anything but thank you… and you know what this means to me. Coming here, as I did—

She is not able to go on but she holds out her hand to them.

Thank you.

RUFUS: [*with real sincerity*] As for my son, I, too, say 'Thank you'. He has good colleagues.

RUFUS claps BERNIE on the shoulder and BERNIE all but collapses under the honour and weight. JOCK turns very brisk and efficient.

JOCK: We're near an hour behind.

Obediently they start out.

You wouldn't have entered the quotes yet, Miss Jenny? Two jobs have come up this morning.

RUFUS: Well, we still have some business!

JENNY: I'll come down and get them, Mr MacDonald.

She goes out with JOCK followed by BERNIE, CHRISTY bringing up the rear, but still audible as he goes downstairs.

CHRISTY: Next time there's a piece of business like that to be done, Jock, you'd better leave it to me. You're a well meaning fellow, but you just haven't got the experience. I knew a feller once—a big fat feller—his aunt used to keep a pie stall in Hobart—

Alone RUFUS stands looking after them for a moment. He glances down at JENNY's desk where her handkerchief is lying beside her typewriter. On an impulse he picks it up, raises it to his nostrils, sniffs approvingly at the perfume, drops it back. He pulls out his heavy watch, snaps it open, looks at the time reprovingly, crosses and goes into his own office. He sits at his desk. The stage is empty for a minute. Then there is the sound of someone running upstairs and KINGSLEY MYERS, carrying a newspaper, comes in buoyantly. He is followed in by GWYNNE, looking very

ACT THREE

pretty in her long riding skirt and wide brimmed hat strapped under her chin.

KINGSLEY: Good morning, sir… a very good morning, sir, and congratulations—all the congratulations in the world! I've never read a better statement—put my own views exactly, but a thousand times better than I could do it myself…

RUFUS sits at his desk with a sheaf of papers in his hand which he is tapping, to give the impression of a man held up in his work.

… with more breadth and clarity, if you know what I mean. Sometimes I'm not very clear—

RUFUS: [*acidly*] I have noticed that tendency, Kingsley. [*Surprised*] You here, too, Gwynne.

GWYNNE: Yes, Mr Torrent. You see, we got the 'Argus' so much earlier and I knew that Kingsley didn't see it until later, and how much this meant to him, I got so awfully excited when I saw the paper that I—I just saddled Rainbird and rode straight over to his place to show him.

RUFUS: Hmmmmm. How's your mother?

GWYNNE: [*knowing quite well what he means*] Not very pleased. And Father's away.

RUFUS: [*non-committal*] Hmmmmm.

GWYNNE: [*daring him*] Both Father and Mother are a little behind the times, Mr Torrent. They haven't quite realised that the New Woman is so much more independent than the old!

They both look at her, KINGSLEY *admiringly,* RUFUS *amazed. Then* RUFUS *shoots a glance of cold suspicion at* JENNY'*s desk.*

KINGSLEY: It was wonderful of you to do it, Gwynne. And wonderful again, sir, for you to—

RUFUS: [*cutting him short*] The credit's Ben's—he wrote it!

KINGSLEY: But where is Ben?

JENNY comes in looking surprised to see them.

Jenny—where's Ben?

JENNY: Downstairs…

A great relief shows for a moment on RUFUS' *face.*

… seeing Mr MacDonald about some page proofs…

KINGSLEY: I've got to see him. We've just been telling Mr Torrent what a wonderful thing he's done with this…

RUFUS: [*waving paper*] And I've just been telling them—the credit belongs to Ben.

KINGSLEY: [*laughing*] Come, sir—now you're being too modest. Everyone knows that not a line goes into the 'Argus' that you haven't approved. Believe me, you'll go down in the history of this district as a man of vision. Oh, come on, Gwynne—we must find Ben.

Taking her he starts to hurry her off… stops for a moment to look at JENNY.

And you, Jenny—I'd risk a bet that you had a hand in this, too.

He practically drags GWYNNE *out, calling 'Ben! Ben!'*

RUFUS: Have you the grace to blush?

She sits demurely at her desk. He towers over her.

A man of vision! Never before has a man been so trapped into such an undeserved reputation!

JENNY: I don't think that matters, Mr Torrent—so long as you're big enough to wear it well.

KINGSLEY *comes back, arms linked with a slightly stiff backed* BEN. GWYNNE *following, smiling.*

KINGSLEY: Hail the conquering hero! Ben, it was hair-raising! Your father told me—

BEN: I can imagine what my father told you, King. My father bears no responsibility. No-one bears any responsibility, except me. It was a stroke of—of mad—

RUFUS: [*genially, yet warning* BEN *to be discreet*] Genius, Ben—genius.

BEN: I am not worthy of your sarcasm, sir… [*Very stiff*] Soon I will be leaving Koolgalla, and—

RUFUS: [*cutting in*] My dear Ben, I am in earnest. Kingsley and Gwynne have come into town especially to congratulate you, to say what we all feel—that with this editorial, you have made the technical position and the future hope clear in the mind of the common man.

KINGSLEY: [*in complete misunderstanding*] Your father is taking no

ACT THREE

part of the credit due. He is leaving it all to you. He is proud of you, Ben. And so are we!

BEN: I don't deserve it, King—the credit shouldn't be mine. There is someone else...

He looks at JENNY *and she shakes her head almost imperceptibly.*

KINGSLEY: Of course, I realise that this is not the end of the battle. The 'Argus' will have to meet so many attacks. So often, you and Ben will feel that your courage has been wasted. But there are more people than you know who feel as I do—and we will be with you. And we'll take care of the soil. I tell you, there are strange new wonderful things going to happen in farming. The day will come when farming will be as exact a science as mathematics, and Koolgalla will be a great city!

RUFUS: I'm glad you realise that it won't be easy. There will be incompetence and self interest and—worst of all—indifference to fight.

GWYNNE: [*unexpectedly*] Kingsley can fight, too! So can I!

Everyone looks at her—she looks back without blushes.

RUFUS: At least, we know those who will be for or against us. We know the town. And if you have to fight, then it is common sense to choose your battleground.

He looks at JENNY *and drops his head in the faintest mocking acknowledgement.*

KINGSLEY: Well, sir, with you and Ben here—

BEN: Don't count on me, King. I may not be here.

RUFUS, *who has lost interest in the conversation and has picked up some papers from* JENNY'*s table and is glancing through them, turns, surprised.* JENNY *and* GWYNNE *both look from one to the other and back at him.* KINGSLEY *is too absorbed at take it seriously.* BEN, *who has said it mainly for its effect on* JENNY, *declines to say more.*

KINGSLEY: You'll be here. You know, this feels like my birthday! Come, Ben—I'll buy you a beer...

BEN *shudders a little but does his best to look nonchalant under* JENNY'*s eye.*

[*More hesitantly to* RUFUS] I don't suppose I could persuade you, sir—

RUFUS: I never drink beer at this hour of the morning...

    KINGSLEY *slightly crushed.*

... only port—as a matter of policy. And it might be good policy to be seen in town this morning.

    Reaches hat from peg.

JENNY: If you will hand me my hat, as well, Mr Torrent, I will slip around the corner and see if Mrs Hartman has prepared the list of her expected guests at her floral festival.

    With a little bow, RUFUS *hands her hat first and she pins it on. They stand aside to allow* JENNY *to precede them.*

RUFUS: It's a sad pity that the ladies can't join us, Kingsley.

    They laugh at this preposterous notion.

JENNY: [*as she goes*] Don't tempt me, gentlemen—I might put your tolerance to the test.

    They sober—she might. BEN *is about to follow them out when* GWYNNE *says...*

GWYNNE: May I speak to you alone for a moment, Ben, if King and your father will excuse us.

    KINGSLEY *looks back wistfully.*

KINGSLEY: Thank you for coming for me, Gwynne... Ben will be seeing you home.

GWYNNE: [*with a brave effort*] I am going to my sister's for lunch. But afterwards—would you ride home with me, King?

KINGSLEY: [*delighted but puzzled*] I—I shall be only too happy, Gwynne... that is, if Ben—

GWYNNE: I have asked you, Kingsley.

KINGSLEY: [*after an embarrassed look at* BEN *and* RUFUS] Th—thank you, Gwynne I shall call for you. [*To* RUFUS] Shall we go, sir?

RUFUS: [*dryly*] It may be as well.

    After a shrewd glance at GWYNNE *and* BEN, RUFUS *goes out followed by* KINGSLEY.

ACT THREE 55

BEN: [*very busy sorting blocks out on the table*] You're very strange this morning, Gwynne.
GWYNNE: It's been a very strange morning. Is it true about what you said, Ben, about not being here?
BEN: [*who hasn't meant it*] Now, look Gwynne—just because a man says something vague, there's no need for you to get upset—
GWYNNE: I'm not upset, Ben.

He looks. By heaven, she isn't.

It suits me very well. But I thought you might be going because of me, and I want you to know that you don't have to go—or stay—because of me any more.

She takes off her glove and slips off her engagement ring.

Take it, Ben...

She looks at the ring before she presses it into his hand.

It was your mother's, wasn't it? Don't give it away so lightly next time.
BEN: [*embarrassed—and genuinely ashamed of hurting her*] My dear, you mustn't do this—
GWYNNE: Do you love me, Ben?
BEN: You—you know how fond I am of you. We played together as kids—we've been friends for years. Everything has always been planned—
GWYNNE: [*insistently*] Do you love me, Ben?
BEN: [*meaning to reassure her*] Of course, I—

Under her eyes his own drop away. He is silent.

GWYNNE: I knew the answer—I've known it for a long time though. But it was hard to face. But this morning, when everything seemed to be changing—Are you in love with Jenny, Ben?
BEN: [*not answering that*] I could live happily with you, Gwynne.
GWYNNE: You could fill in the hours between morning and night... This way is best. And it's not so bad, now that it's out and over. I expect I gave you up a long time ago. I imagine I'll always feel rather sentimental about you... I don't suppose you'll ever grow old for me, and I don't suppose that the woman you do marry will

ever seem quite worthy of you—no matter how superior to you she may be.

BEN *is feeling the nostalgia of parting and he is nearer to being interested in* GWYNNE *than he has been before.*

But now that I have faced it, I find there are compensations. You'll be an awful handful for somebody, Ben—perhaps, in a way, I feel rather relieved...

BEN'*s jaw drops. Then he has the grace to laugh.*

BEN: Well—that takes the edge off my noble shame!

She picks up her gloves, starts to put them on before leaving.

Gwynne, will you give King a chance later? You know how much he cares.

GWYNNE: I know. I expect I will—later. I like him very much—and next time, I think I'd be rather more loved than loving. And next time a marriage is arranged for me—I shall arrange it myself!

She goes over to JENNY'*s piece of mirror, and begins to adjust her hat, settling the strap under her chin.*

BEN: Did you leave Rainbird at the stables?

GWYNNE: [*at mirror*] Yes...

BEN: I'll come down with you.

GWYNNE: [*turning around*] Just as far as the door.

BEN: [*appreciating her*] Gwynne, you are so sweet—and I do feel a cad.

GWYNNE: Ben, you are so charming—and keep away from me in the future, please. As for being a cad, I'm beginning to think that it's better to be a cad than a fool. Perhaps if we had more cads and fewer fools, we'd have fewer tragedies, too—in the end.

She nods dismissal to him as JENNY *is heard on the stairs.*

BEN: That doesn't sound like you, Gwynne.

GWYNNE: You forget—I've known Jenny, too.

GWYNNE *smiles at the puzzled* JENNY *and goes out.* JENNY *shrugs her bewilderment. She goes to her desk shakes her head at its confusion and begins to tidy it.*

ACT THREE

BEN: [*imperiously*] Jenny. I want to talk to you.
JENNY: [*dropping blocks*] And I want to talk to you. Ben, forgive me for putting that editorial in. As it happens, everything has turned out well, but still it was—well—unforgivable. It was so right—and it said things so necessary to say— Oh, Ben, I couldn't help myself! Mind you, I'd probably do it again tomorrow, but I do feel ashamed of myself for having done it yesterday!
BEN: [*with a crack of laughter*] Oh, Jenny, my Jenny!
JENNY: Perhaps your father is right after all—women are too emotional. Anyway, if you had done the right thing and put it in yourself... [*Laughs*] But I did leave the explanation... and my resignation—on your father's desk.
BEN: Protection for the weaker element.
JENNY: I didn't think you were weak Ben—not really.
BEN: [*close to her*] Didn't you, Jenny?

> *He comes close to her. She wants to avoid what she can see coming.*

JENNY: You're just beginning to grow up, Ben. Just beginning to become a wonderful, strong, fine exciting man... That's why...
BEN: [*taking her hands*] Why—what, Jenny?
JENNY: Why I think you ought to go away from here.
BEN: Well, thank you. I had no idea I was becoming such a burden to my friends.
JENNY: [*she has no time for this sort of coquetry*] Don't be silly—you know how much I'll hate to see you go. But you need to do it, Ben—you have said yourself so often that you live in your father's shadow.
BEN: [*waving it away*] Pardonable rhetoric. And don't be too bitter about the old boy—I know he hasn't been quite straight over this editorial, but—
JENNY: You do talk the most arrant nonsense, Ben. Your father is a wonderful man—
BEN: In his way—
JENNY: [*sailing on*] Where do you think you got your intelligence... [*Grudging*]... and charm and that blind instinct for the right road to follow? He has something else, Ben—a consciousness of being

alone, of pain and struggle that you haven't learned. That has given him maturity.

BEN: I can learn, Jenny.

JENNY: Not in Koolgalla where he will always lead the way.

BEN: You're right, of course. You are, always.

JENNY: Are you a good sailor?

BEN: [*grinning*] No.

JENNY: Then that's the thing for you. Ben, you have to attempt the things that don't come easily to you—the things you don't do well. Otherwise you'll always be Ben Torrent, drifting in his father's shadow, and not big enough to cast one of his own. You're like this town—this town that has to choose between digging up its good earth for the chance of gold or planting it with the certainty of fruit trees. You are like that—you—and this town and the world beyond us, perhaps…

They turn, MANSON, *now calm, is standing in the doorway.*

MANSON: Interrupting something?

They look at him with hostile eyes.

I left in a hurry before—I'm a man whose temper bolts with him sometimes. And yet I'm as easy as a lamb to live with. [*To* JENNY] Would you think that?

JENNY: It isn't one of the things I'd think about at all!

MANSON: You don't like me, do you? Pity—Torrent scored there, when he brought you here to work.

JENNY *goes into* RUFUS' *office—she is listening, although she closes the door.*

BEN: Do you wish to see my father?

MANSON: No, I want to see you. I've seen your father already. Nothing's changed there! I said I'd fight him to the end, and I will! And I'll enjoy it! When I fight I don't spare myself—or my money. This town won't die—it'll grow.

BEN: In the way Kingsley prophesied—

MANSON: That's likely.

BEN: And wouldn't the joke be on you, Mr Manson?

MANSON: Don't you believe it, boy. You'll never find all my eggs in

ACT THREE

one basket! I've taken the bulk of my money out of gold years ago. It's here and there—some of it's in land. If Myers' scheme does work, I'll be the one making money out of it! That's looking ahead, Ben. And I'm looking ahead too, when I say this town can do with another newspaper! Like to be an editor, Ben? I'm making you an offer.

BEN: To fight my own father!

MANSON: [*shrewdly*] Wouldn't you like to? Don't be ashamed of it, Ben. It's the law of nature. The young bulls have to fight the old ones for their rights of leadership. I'd give you a free hand—more or less. Think it over. If you make up your mind quickly, you'll find me in the Horseshoe Bar at the Royal. If Rufus Torrent's to be seen drinking in the morning and playing the King of Ireland—by heaven, so am I!

> MANSON *goes out with a wave of his hand.* JENNY *comes from the inner office.* BEN, *almost duplicating* RUFUS' *earlier movement, has moved to the window and is looking down on the town.*

JENNY: [*after a pause*] Is this your chance, Ben?
BEN: You heard?
JENNY: [*nods, then says truthfully*] I was listening.
BEN: It could be—if I could give myself a good reason for taking it... if you can give it to me. Jenny, will you marry me?
JENNY: [*pale with emotion and responsibility*] No, Ben.
BEN: I'm sorry—I thought you cared for me.
JENNY: I do—I like you very much, Ben. But I don't want to spend the rest of my life looking after a man.
BEN: I had forgotten. The—new—woman...
JENNY: [*serenely—here she is untouchable now*] The new woman... who will marry and have children and look after them... not baby a husband, as so many have done in the past.
BEN: [*really hurt*] I thought—you said that I could be something better.
JENNY: [*understanding his hurt*] You will be, Ben—but not with me. I should simply take the place of your father in your life. And I should become a bitter, criticising, domineering woman. You wouldn't wish to ruin me, Ben. And that would be real ruin. Not your lending library word—real ruin.

BEN *starts across the room as though to go, then unable to leave it alone, comes back.*

BEN: Is that the real reason you won't marry me?

JENNY: It's enough. But apart from that...

BEN: Apart from that... ?

JENNY: I think I'm going to marry your father!

BEN *is completely breathless. She walks back to her desk and he follows her.*

BEN: Did you say... ?

She nods.

But, Jenny—why?

JENNY: Because I like him. Because he's proud and stiff-necked and adult—but carries within him always a young and desperate boy from Dublin, whom no-one has ever comforted. You don't know that boy, my comfortable Ben—he suffered that you should live without making his acquaintance... but I have been poor, I have found the world against me, and I shall find my way to his heart.

BEN: Frankly, I don't understand a word of it—except that he's old enough to be my father!

JENNY: [*tartly*] Well, he isn't mine! [*Then repentant*] Oh, Ben, dear Ben, forgive me if I've hurt you. You'll be glad—eventually.

He looks at her—he knows better. She is deeply troubled.

Now that I've told you how I feel—what are you going to do? [*Hesitantly*] Take Manson's offer?

BEN: To fight my father?

She nods, afraid of words.

No—I'm not big enough... yet! If someday I have to match Rufus Torrent, it will be the meeting of equals. I won't be a weapon in another man's hands.

Suddenly RUFUS *is heard on the stairs.*

RUFUS: [*off*] Right, Jock—bring them to the office in half an hour—

JENNY: [*in an urgent whisper*] No bitterness, Ben—

BEN: No bitterness, Jenny. But he must have realised how I felt about you. He might have told me that you—and he—

ACT THREE

JENNY: He doesn't know about it—yet, Ben—

    RUFUS *comes in carrying the aura of a couple of morning ports.*

RUFUS: [*affably*] What the devil are you doing, lounging round the office, Ben. Kingsley is waiting for you.

BEN: I am about to join him, sir—But I would like to speak to you for a moment—

    JENNY *is in a panic.* RUFUS *stops on his way to the office.*

RUFUS: I have been trying to get into this office all the morning, Ben—people keep running in and out. [*To* JENNY] I'm not in to callers for the rest of the morning.

JENNY: [*her eyes on* BEN] No, sir.

BEN: Just one thing, Father—do you realise that we are both taking credit that we don't deserve—you for publishing views you would never have countenanced—

    JENNY *stops a gesture of protest half way.*

Me, for holding views I did not dare to express. And all the time, the person who dared everything—took every chance—sits there...

    RUFUS *looks over his shoulder to make sure* JENNY *is sitting there.*

And the credit goes to those who least deserve it.

RUFUS: Of course, Ben, if you're going to spend your life making sure that credit for change goes where it's due, you'll never have time to make the change. And that would be a pity, now, wouldn't it? For what are the saints and the heroes but the vision and the sword of the common rest of us. And who cares, in the long breadth of the years who dreamed the dream, so long as the common rest of us made it come true?

    JENNY *is looking at him and* BEN, *seeing her look, catches his breath, understanding. But* RUFUS *is looking far away.*

BEN: But Father, Jenny—

RUFUS: Jenny is more of a damned fool than I think if she cares for anything less than the achievement. She understands.

    RUFUS *is finished with all this talk. He makes for his office, saying over his shoulder.*

I have a meeting I must attend after lunch, Ben, and I want to do tomorrow's editorial before I go—a follow up on the morning's...

He hesitates, turns.

I would like your advice, Ben.

BEN: [*appreciating this from* RUFUS] Thank you, Father. Always at your disposal. But I am sure that you are more able than I am... in everything.

His eyes are on JENNY.

RUFUS: [*carelessly*] Probably—but no-one can say that I don't ask for advice.

He goes into his office, slamming the door. He sits at desk, picks *up some proofs, starts to write something.* BEN *looks at* JENNY.

BEN: I can see there is nothing for you but that.

He gets his hat from the rack.

RUFUS: [*from office*] Jenny!

She turns to look at door with a sparkle in her face. She collects her pad and pencil and starts for the door. Half way there, she turns. On an impulse, but with no hint of coquetry, she kisses her fingers to BEN, *looking at him sorrowfully, affectionately.*

[*Very loudly*] Jenny!

She moves to door of the office. BEN *moves to downstairs exit. They turn and look back at each other.* JENNY *has her hand on the door knob.* BEN *is looking back.* RUFUS *flings open the office door.*

JENNY!! I WANT YOU!!

JENNY: Yes sir!

RUFUS *turns back into office.*

BEN: [*lovingly and sadly and quizzically*] Goodbye, Mama—

One more smile, each to each, and JENNY *is going into the office.* BEN *is still watching her go as...*

FINAL CURTAIN

ALSO AVAILABLE FROM CURRENCY PRESS

Plays of the 50s, Volume 1
Edited by Katharine Brisbane
The authors in this volume are the precursors of an Australian theatre beginning to be heard in the post-war period, at a time when material prosperity was overshadowed by the threat of the Cold War, and Australians were increasingly daunted by the challenges of mass immigration, the Korean War and what came to be known as 'the cultural cringe'. These playwrights of the 1940s and 50s made their own theatre: for the poet Douglas Stewart it was myth-making verse tragedy in *Shipwreck*; for social-realist Oriel Gray it was *Sky Without Birds*, a drama about tolerance and growing up; Ralph Peterson's *Night of the Ding Dong* punctured the pretensions of his forefathers; and Ric Throssell, at the centre of Australian politics, confronted Australians with the consequences of atomic war with *The Day Before Tomorrow*. These plays helped to create the groundswell that led to public demand for our own Australian theatre.
ISBN 978 0 86819 627 5

Plays of the 50s Volume 2
Edited by Katharine Brisbane
The exhilaration caused by the success in 1955 of *The Doll* galvanised a host of new playwrights. Among them was Barbara Vernon, whose *The Multi-Coloured Umbrella* (1957) a drama of the racetrack, exploits the novelty of an irredeemably Australian way of life. Peter Kenna in his comedy-drama *The Slaughter of St Teresa's Day* (1959), introduces the first of his Irish-Australian matriarchs, Oola Maguire. In *Image in the Clay* (1960) David Ireland blends realism and poetry in his stark portrait of a rural Aboriginal family. And, most radically, Ray Mathew in *The Life of the Party* (1960) draws a desperate portrait of post-war urban sophisticates trapped in the shadow of the Cold War. Exploring a new theatre distanced from European realism, these plays mark a journey towards a recognisably Australian rhythmic form and a more poetic, visceral drama characteristic of the theatre later in the century.
ISBN 978 0 86819 695 4

Belonging: Australian playwriting in the 20th century
John McCallum

Belonging explores the relationship between 20th century Australian playwriting and a developing concept of nation. Play by play the author builds a history that shows the creative tension between nationalism and cosmopolitanism; high art and larrikin populism; representational realism and adventurous modernism. He looks also at the interaction between the personal and the political and the ambivalence between affection and aggression of much Australian humour.

Belonging is the most comprehensive account of 20th century Australian playwriting ever written. McCallum's research and narrative skills combine to give us a perceptive overview of the major writers and their works and bring to life many others that have been forgotten. As he teases out the different themes and styles that have played out on our stages, the author explores how Australian playwrights sought to define their place in the world. The search to belong, he argues, was a major preoccupation of their work.

From of the finest scholars of Australian playwriting, this authoritative study is a starting point for anyone who wants to understand the relationship between our drama and our sense of self or who is simply keen to learn about a particular play or author.

ISBN 978 0 86819 658 9

For these and other titles, as well as teachers' notes, critical essays, author interviews and other resources, please visit our website:
www.currency.com.au

www.ingramcontent.com/pod-product-compliance
Lightning Source LLC
Chambersburg PA
CBHW050021090426
42734CB00021B/3368